Make Your Own Soap

Also by Dorothy Richter

FELLS GUIDE TO HAND PUPPETS

MAKE YOUR OWN
SOAP
PLAIN AND FANCY

DOROTHY RICHTER

ILLUSTRATED BY THE AUTHOR

DOLPHIN BOOKS

DOUBLEDAY & COMPANY, INC.

GARDEN CITY, NEW YORK

1974

ISBN: 0-385-01776-6
Library of Congress Catalog Card Number 73–83663
9 8 7 6 5 4 3 2

To Eliza
for her help and encouragement

Contents

Acknowledgments

In writing this book I have incurred a debt of gratitude to many people; to the friends who joined in the search for casting materials and those who brought soap dishes, antique soap carvings, and soap mitts; to the sculptor who carved the soap head; the friend who suffered through my illegible penmanship to type the manuscript; the photographer; and the friends who posed for photographs.

Grateful acknowledgment is made to Penwalt Corporation, writer Roberta Kenyon, and the University of Vermont, Extension Division.

Preface: Why Make Soap?

I had never given much thought to soap. One tends to take for granted any readily available necessity. I kept a supply on hand; that is, when I remembered to add it to the grocery list.

That was the extent of my concern with soap until I wrote a feature article on an elderly couple (the Disterhafts) who supplemented their income by making and selling two and a half tons of soap a year. I admit I went for the interview with no greater interest than to wonder why they chose to make soap instead of something simple, such as pot holders.

Mr. D. had agreed to make a batch of soap to demonstrate how it was done. When I arrived he was sitting on a bench in the back yard mixing the lye and water solution. The fat had been melted and was cooling. When both ingredients reached the proper temperature (this was determined by feeling the outside of each container) they were combined.

At this point the result was a gray greasy mess, but as he slowly stirred, the mixture began to lighten. After half an hour of stirring he poured forty pounds of creamy, white, honey-thick soap into a large flat metal pan. It looked good enough to eat, but that wasn't what was exciting me. I was thinking of the soap carving one could make from a large block of soap. In my art classes, we were confined to the size of a bar of Ivory Soap. Carving soap was often a frustrating experience because of the tendency of the soap to chip. Using homemade soap, the carving could be done before the prolonged drying period, when the soap is much more pliant.

Mr. D. broke into my reverie with, "Tomorrow it will be set enough to cut into bars, then it must cure. After several weeks it will be ready to use." My interest in soap was aroused. I learned that tallow was the fat used. It was donated by the owner of a market. Fat, generally considered a waste product, is easy to get. A meat market is Mr. D.'s only source of supply. However, when the project was in its infancy, reclaimed kitchen grease was used.

I was impressed by the simple equipment—a six-gallon stone jar, a sawed-off broom handle for stirring, a large shallow metal pan (a cardboard box would serve the purpose), and a large kettle in which to melt tallow. The ingredients for soap were also few and inexpensive —fat and lye. The fat was free; the lye purchased by the case.

The only advertising done by the D.'s was to cut a forty-pound batch of soap into small bars and distribute them to friends and acquaintances. Word-of-mouth advertising did the rest. They could sell more soap than time or energy permit them to make. Orders come from churches, fraternal organizations, and gift shops. But the bulk of their soap is sold at out-of-doors produce markets, sometimes called flea markets or green markets. Mrs. D. has added aprons and pickles to their specialty. With the growing interest in the homely arts, the D.'s take their place at craft fairs along with candlemakers, creative embroiderers, and potters.

I attended a nearby flea market to learn who bought homemade soap and why. There was a stream of customers to the soap booth. Six-pound packages of powdered soap were being sold for use in automatic washing machines. Most of the soap would be used for laundering clothes, but there were several people who had other uses for it. One woman said it is an excellent dog shampoo and discourages fleas; a barber buys it to use as a shaving soap; another customer said it is the only thing that controls the rash on his legs; a doctor prescribes it for patients with poison ivy. The growing awareness of water-polluting phosphates in commercial cleansers is making soap converts of many women. One woman told me it gave her great satisfaction to know that she was not contributing to water pollution. "I don't even have a wrapper to throw away," she said.

The day I posted the article on the D.'s soapmaking I turned soapmaker, making blocks from which I carved animals, heads, and figures. As an art medium the soap was everything I hoped it would be.

Next I turned to making toilet soap, prompted by the following article, "Soap Is Soap—or Is It?" by Roberta Kenyon as it appeared in the May 14, 1972, View of Wisconsin of the *Appleton-Post Crescent* Sunday newspaper:

"It used to be that a bar of soap made suds so that the dirt on your hands or body would slip off and the suds would leave a fragrant scent. It was good soap.

A baby could be cleansed with it. But between the time when baby was little and the present, something happened. It was not good.

"Competition began to destroy our confidence in that bar of soap that made baby's skin glow. Competition began to reshape it, to strengthen it and finally to put additives to it. One was to make your skin softer. Another was to remove perspiration. Another was to restore the glow to your skin. You would become ageless.

"Instead, what happened? Heretofore, you trooped nonchalantly to the store. When you got there, you happily had to decide whether you should buy the soap that made your skin ageless. Or did you want a soap that would not make you 'offend'? What to buy? Should you buy the pink bar, the curved one, the square one? Which one? No longer did you even consider the baby soap, the soap that years ago did not damage your skin. Now you had become a sophisticated and picky soap buyer. You would look for the soap that would not allow you to offend and would still let you smell clean and would also make you ageless. So you stocked your shelves. What happened?

"The scientists came into the picture. It was discovered that the soap that does not allow you to 'offend' is loaded with a chemical that does harm to the skin and if used for too long a time may even damage your brain tissues. It was hinted that the soap containing this chemical should be put on a prescription basis! So you throw out that soap and confidently begin to use the one that would make you ageless. What happened?

"The chemical in this lovely scented bar is said by scientists to contain an anti-bacterial chemical. If you used the soap for any length of time you would become allergic to sunlight!

"Now, more perplexed than ever, comes the dawn. Which soap, then, should you use? You've lost your desire to become ageless. You've decided that to 'offend' might be better than to become mentally deficient. So now another problem looms. You don't have a grandma. You're positive Mother doesn't have any answers. Therefore, does anybody know how to make 'home-made' soap?"

I had an idea that the author of the article was one of thousands of perplexed women who had come to the conclusion that the only soap in which they could have confidence was soap they themselves made. I decided to provide them with a recipe.

A good friend who is a librarian, offered to research for me and soon I was launched on the making of toilet soap—safe, pure superfatted toilet soap. I had no idea of the countless hours I would spend in the kitchen experimenting with recipes, using this ingredient, discarding that. Nor did I realize how making toilet soap would lead to decorating gift soap and boxes, making ceramic dishes and hand-printed paper. But my enthusiasm increased with each successful experiment. When at last I concluded that the experiments must end and the writing begin, I had made sixty-nine batches of toilet soap.

This book is the result of my research and experiments with soap as a creative medium and as a safe and sane cleansing agent.

1. A Short History of Soap

No one knows when soap was first discovered. In the most remote periods it appears that clothes were cleaned by being rubbed or stamped upon in water without the addition of any substance whatsoever.

Probably the oldest literary reference to soap is found in the four-thousand-year-old clay tablets written by the Mesopotamians. One such recipe called for 1 part of oil to 5½ parts of potash. A much more complicated recipe required Myrtle root, pulverized fir bark, powdered rosin, alkali ash, barley, the skin of a water snake, and several other ingredients. When properly prepared and applied as directed, this recipe not only cured the patient but made him smell better. The latter might appear to be the more difficult accomplishment considering the lack of regard for cleanliness. It is generally conceded that these first mixtures were either hair pomades or ointments to be rubbed upon the body, as the ancients did not understand the art of producing soap in a dry solid form. Also, the discovery of soap and the discovery of its washing properties were not simultaneous.

Pliny the Elder, the noted Roman scholar of the first century A.D., observed that soap was first used externally as a medicine, being of benefit in the dis-

3

posal of scrofulous sores. He also noted that the pomades used by the Germans to color their hair were
imported by Rome for use by fashionable ladies and
the gallants. In the second century A.D., Galen, the
famous physician, recommended soap for the removal of
dirt from clothes and bodies, but the general use of
soap was not a reality for several hundred years. It is
reasonable to suppose that the first pomades used by
the Egyptians were rubbed upon their bodies as a protection from the sun.

Before the discovery of soap as a cleansing agent,
primitive people of many lands had been using natural soaps, the juices from saponaceous plants, seeds,
roots, barks, leaves, and fruits. Some are still in use
today. As an experiment, bruise the leaves of the
common wild pink known as "bouncing bet" between
your fingers or two stones, then rub them in water to
get a fine lather. This serves very well as soap.

On the western plains, the Spanish bayonet or yucca
plants were used to make soap. In tropical America,
the soapberry tree supplies soap. The fine bubbly lather
comes from the pulp of the fruit. An excellent soap
comes from the soapbark tree of Chili. It is imported
into the United States to be used in cosmetics, shaving
cream, and dentifrices. These plants all contain a
substance known as saponen, which contains neither
alkali nor grease, the principal ingredients of soap.
Chemists have not been able to duplicate saponen.

Of the plants with a saponaceous juice, the ancients
used at least one. They also used an earthy alkali
called niter, similar to carbonate of soda, and fuller's
earth, which had the characteristics of both marl and

4

soapstone. Foul-smelling animal bile was also used to wash clothes.

The cheapest, however, and the most common article used to wash garments was the urine of men and animals. The alkali separated when the urine became old. The alkalized urine was warmed and used to wash greasy clothes. To procure a supply of it, the washers placed vessels at street corners. When they were filled by passers-by they were removed. One chronicler observed, "The practice of having such conveniences was certainly more decent than that of employing the walls of churches and other buildings. At Rome, that which at present spoils and renders filthy was converted to use." Perhaps this is the earliest example of recycling. The clothes washed with urine were trod upon with the feet. Because of the foul smell, washers in Rome were obliged to live either in the suburbs or in some unfrequented streets.

Long before soap was discovered, the Egyptians and other civilized peoples made a fetish of bathing. They washed before and after meals. Before baths, they were rubbed down with sand to cleanse the pores. This was followed by a thorough washing and laving with perfumed oils. Faces and heads were shaved, body hair removed every ten days.

When the Romans became virtually the rulers of the civilized world, they were determined to enjoy all of the esthetic pleasures of the Hellenic and Oriental peoples they had conquered. The elaborate Roman baths contained hot and cold rooms, warm plunge baths, frigid baths, exercise rooms, and steam rooms. The final room was for massage. The body was rubbed with perfumed oil after the skin was scraped with a strigil, an instrument of bone or metal resembling a shoehorn. The Romans were, no doubt, reasonably clean without the use of soap by virtue of long soaking and arduous scraping.

In all probability, the discovery of soap was an accident as so many discoveries have been. Some historians believe the cleansing properties of soap were discovered in Rome about one thousand B.C. Legend has it that on a hillside outside of Rome the poor people sacrificed animals to the gods by burning them on a crude altar. The animal fat accumulated at the base of the altar and mixed with the ashes from the fires. Rain washed this mixture down the hillside to the clay banks of the Tiber where women pounded the dirt from garments. They discovered that by rubbing this mixture into their clothes the clothes became cleaner with less effort. The place where this happened was a hill named Sapo. It was Pliny the Elder who named this concoction "Sapo," the word from which soap was derived. The word Sapo can be seen in the word soap in every modern European language. The Italians call it *sapone*; the French, *savon*; the Dutch, *sepo*; the Hungarians call it *szappan*.

Others think soap may have been discovered as a body cleanser when a Gaul who had rubbed goat fat and beechwood ashes into his hair in an effort to make himself especially attractive before attending a festival got caught in the rain and was thereby treated to an unexpected shampoo.

There is no evidence to indicate that soap as a cleansing agent was in use in biblical times, though there are at least two references to the word "soap" in the Scriptures.

A few years after the Romans discovered the cleansing qualities of soap, they began making it commercially. In the ruins of Pompeii, the Roman city swallowed up by the eruption of Vesuvius in A.D. 79, a soapmaker's shop and a quantity of soap were found among the ruins. The knowledge of soapmaking was spread far and wide by the Romans.

On the Iberian peninsula in the district later known as Castile, cosmetics, soap, and ointments were made from the oil of ripe olives. By the seventh century soapmaking was an important industry in Italy. Soapmakers organized craft guilds to uphold standards and protect members. Marseille, France, was one of the earliest soapmaking centers in western Europe. Olive oil replaced the goat tallow used by the Gauls. The superior quality of this soap gave Marseille supremacy from A.D. 800 to 1200. In the thirteenth century Savona and Venice became important centers of soapmaking. In ancient Castile, craftsmen made such a fine soap that the name still denotes a superior soap. The English started making soap as early as 1200. It was turned out in Bristol, Coventry, and London. Later it became a leading industry.

The processing of soap came to an abrupt end with the advent of the Dark Ages, when the Roman Empire was conquered by the Goths and other barbaric tribes in the fifth century. After the fall of the Roman Empire, the knowledge of soapmaking was temporarily lost to the world. Civilization stepped back in time. Dirt and filth reigned supreme in Europe through the Dark and Middle Ages (500–1500). This was the time of the great unwashed, and as a consequence plague after plague swept through the crowded cities leaving millions dead. It was no coincidence that these epidemics occurred when living conditions were at the lowest hygienic level. But the obvious connection between filth and the Black Death escaped medieval churchmen, who considered the unwashed state to be a proper mortification of the flesh! Saint Jerome stated, "A clean body and a clean dress mean an unclean soul." The "mortification" must have been overpowering when a congregation of foul-smelling creatures who hoped by virtue of their unwashed, vermin-infested bodies and clothing to pass through the pearly gates. As a safeguard against disease, oranges with the pulp removed and replaced by a sponge soaked in vinegar or even garlic juice which gave off a strong aroma were carried by every doctor, clergyman, and merchant whose occupations took them into disease-ridden areas. Others covered their nostrils with rags soaked in vinegar. Henry IV banished the orange in favor of the pomander, a small perforated box containing spices. It was carried around the neck, in the pocket, or in the handle of a walking stick.

An interest in bathing was awakened by the crusaders who returned with tales of oriental perfumed baths. But the lack of sufficient water and the high cost of soap made bathing a rarity to be indulged in only by the wealthy. Queen Elizabeth, according to a chronicler of the times, bathed once a month "whether she needed it or no." Queen Isabella of Spain boasted that she had only two baths in her life—one when she was born and one when she was married. England's Henry IV founded the Order of the Bath in 1399 to encourage his nobles to take at least one bath during their lives—during the ritual of knighthood. One historian writing of medieval times says, ". . . it is only too obvious that under their chain mail the knights were lousy, scrofulous, and thick with grime and antique sweat." The nobility resorted to liberal doses of perfume to mask the offending odor of unwashed bodies.

When Oliver Cromwell (1599–1658) came into power, he opposed the idea of people using soap and imposed severely heavy taxes on the product. The stiff tax prevented the poorer classes from bathing even when they had water to do it. In 1622 King James I granted a monopoly to a soapmaker for $100,000 a year. Later taxes levied in England brought as much into the royal treasury as the equivalent of five million dollars in today's currency. The heavy taxes levied by Cromwell were lifted during the Restoration. It wasn't until 1872 that a tax of a penny a pound was reimposed.

Cleanliness made very little headway until the eighteenth century, the Age of Enlightenment. Gladstone succeeded in having the soap tax abolished saying, "A clean nation is a happy healthy one." An idea long overdue. In 1770 Nicolas Leblanc, a French chemist, discovered that the expensive alkali portion of soap could be manufactured from common salt to form carbonate of soda. Not long afterward another French chemist, Michel Eugene Chevreul, introduced certain kinds of acids to assure precise production control.

But it wasn't until the nineteenth century that the relationship between disease and uncleanliness was made known by Lewis Pasteur (1822–95). He proved that germs were the cause of many communicable diseases and infections. Consequently, improvements in the control of disease took place. Cleanliness came back into fashion. City streets were no longer filthy; underground sewers, cesspools, and public baths were installed, garbage was collected and disposed of.

Though bodily cleanliness wasn't considered necessary in seventeenth-century England, the pilgrims who came to America did their best to adhere to John Wesley's statement, "Cleanliness is indeed next to godliness." It wasn't easy. The crude living conditions made even the simple task of washing the hands a chore. It was a lucky household that possessed pitchers, basins, pails, and tubs. Water was carried in crude, heavy buckets from brooks or lakes before wells were dug. It was a precious commodity, so hands were seldom washed before meals and baths in the winter were infrequent. Water was heated over the open fire. If it remained in the tub overnight, it was sure to freeze. Soap was made out of doors each spring from cooking grease and ashes, saved and stored until the first warm day. The lye was made from ashes. It was combined with the melted grease in an iron kettle over an open fire and stirred until it became thick enough to pour. The difficulty in making soap was in knowing when the lye was of the proper strength. In a recipe of the time housewives were advised, "If your lye will bear an egg or potato so that you can see a piece of the surface as big as a ninepence, it is just enough, but if it sinks below the top of the lye, it is too weak and will never make soap. If it is buoyed up half-way, the lye is too strong and is just as bad."

There were German and Polish soapmakers in Virginia as early as 1608. Their soap was sold by the pound and cut off to order. Few could afford it. The pilgrim women continued to make their own soap until the first sharp businessman saw the possibility of profit by making the rounds of villages offering to take waste household fats in exchange for soap. The women were more than willing to be relieved of the smelly task. By 1671, northern New England's chief income was derived from supplying fats and ashes to soapmakers.

The use of soap was given a boost when Benjamin Franklin imported a small oval French bathtub, the first in America. It was constructed of copper with a built-in grate to heat water.

By 1800 a number of factories were producing soap commercially on the Eastern Seaboard. In 1843 Benjamin Babbitt began manufacturing several varieties of soap. His business expanded rapidly. He was the first to give away samples of soap for advertising purposes, the first to use pictorial advertising, and the first to seek publicity through theaters. His six large kettles for boiling soap had a capacity of 3,500,000 pounds and required $216,000 worth of material to fill.

The Civil War created a shortage of soap. The Union levied a penny a pound tax. So much of the limited supply went to the armed forces that a gift of soap was a prized item. With the close of the Civil War and the boom that followed, the soapmaking industry flourished. Advertising took on a new aspect. Colorful cards dangled from the ceilings of grocery stores extolling the benefits of a variety of soap products. Premium labels could be redeemed for items of value according to advertisements. Glowing endorsements by theater beauties of the day reminded women that beauty such as theirs was but a bar of soap away. One look at Lily Langtree or Lillian Russell with their fancy hair-do's and décolleté gowns, and the product sold.

Family washing was a laborious and time-consuming chore done by hand with the aid of a scrubbing board and wash tubs. This "receet" for washing was written in the 1880s by a mother for her newly married daughter:

1. Bild fire in backyard to hete water, use rain water in iron kettle.
2. Set tubs so wind wont blow smoke in yore eyes if wind is pert.
3. Shave one hole cake of lie soap in bilin' water.
4. Sort close make one pile white close, one pile cullud, one pile britches and rags.
5. Stir flour in cold water tel smooth then thin down with bilin' water.
6. Rub dirty spots on board then bile. Rub cullud spots but don't bile, just rench and starch.
7. Take white things out of kettle with punchier stick then rench blew and starch.
8. Spread tee towels on grass.
9. Hang britches and rags on fence.
10. Pore rench water on flower bed.
11. Scrub porch with sopey water.
12. Turn tubs upside down.
13. Go put on clean dress, smooth hair with side combs, brew a cup of tea. Set and rest and rock a spell and count your blessings.

Various types of hand-propelled machines preceded the mechanical washing machine, which did not come into general popularity until World War I. The heavy wooden boxes in which soap was packed for the market were often used as a platform by street-corner speechmakers, so from this practice the phrase "soap-box orator" emerged. There were a number of other permanent contributions to the English language such as "soft soaping," "soap the way," and "no soap."

We have come a long way since the days when being clean was considered playing into the devil's hands. Cleanliness is now recognized as a morale builder as well as a safeguard to health. Our government officials have decreed that bath and laundry units must accompany each combat division into war. The United States has 90 per cent of all of the bathtubs in the world. An average American uses an estimated twenty-seven pounds of soap per year (bar and liquid) for personal cleanliness, laundry, and other purposes. This is a great contrast to Red China's two ounces per person.

Soap plays a part in nearly every phase of man's civilized existence. If the world's soapmaking plants were shut down, the mortality rate would skyrocket, disease would be rampant, and much of the world's industry would be crippled. It has been said that the level of civilization can be determined more accurately by the amount of soap used than by any other index.

2. All-purpose Soap

You may feel a bit hesitant about making your first batch of soap, but don't; there is no such thing as a failure in soapmaking. Anyone who can read and follow directions can make soap.

Soap is a combination of fats and alkalis. The dirt which we wish to wash from garments is a blend of oil and dust. You can see that if soap has too much fat in it, the fat is added to the oil already in the garment and does not break up into particles which are kept in suspension until washed away.

On the other hand, if the lye that separates the grease has been added too generously, the penetrating factors in its composition eat into the delicate fabric leaving tiny holes in the cloth. For this reason, the lye and fat must be carefully proportioned. When this is done the resulting soap is safe and efficient.

Since the first step in soapmaking is gathering the fat or grease, let us consider the types suitable for soapmaking. The following fats are listed in order of desirability:

Tallow: Beef tallow can be used alone. Mutton tallow makes a soap that is too hard and brittle. About $\frac{1}{5}$ of the total amount of fat may be combined with other fats with satisfactory results.

Lard: Lard is the fat from hogs. A combination of tallow and lard makes the best laundry soap.

Oils: Olive oil, cottonseed oil, castor oil, corn oil, and other vegetable oils in combination with fats make a high-grade soap. Mineral oil will not make soap.

Table Scraps: Fats that have no cooking value can be used in soap. Save meat fryings, rinds, and scraps. They should be free from water since it causes fat to become rancid. Even grease in which onions and fish have been fried can be used if properly treated. Store fats in a cool dry place.

Poultry Fat: This fat can be used in small amounts with other fats. Used alone it makes a soft spongy soap.

Preparing Fats for Soapmaking

Fats may be grouped into two classes:

1. Fats rendered from tallow, meat trimmings, and rinds are ready for soap when they have been cooked down and all of the fat extracted. Tallow should be cut into small chunks for quicker rendering.

   The crisp cracklings that remain, especially those from hog fat, are highly prized by some cooks. In the South, corn bread containing crack-lings is known as crackling bread. They are also ground and sprinkled on toast, or used in cook-ies. Cracklings impart a flavor not duplicated by any other shortening.

2. Fats rendered from meat fryings and other refuse kitchen grease. Fats of this nature must be cleansed of dirt, lean meat, salt, and other impu-rities. This is called washing and is done as fol-lows: Add an equal amount of water to the fat and bring it to the boiling point. Remove it from the fire, stir, and cool slightly. Add cold wa-ter (1 quart to 1 gallon of warm liquid). The cold water precipitates the foreign particles. The fat will collect on the top. When cold, remove the grease from the water and scrape impurities from the bottom of the cake. Melt the cake and repeat the process. Strain through cheesecloth.

To Sweeten Rancid or Sour Fat

Boil the fat in a mixture of vinegar and water, using 1 part vinegar to 5 parts water. Set aside to cool and treat as above after washing.

To Remove Strong Odors

1. Melt the fat and cook it with sour milk (1 cup to a pound of grease).
2. Another method is to cook potatoes in the grease (a medium-size sliced potato for every 3 pounds of grease).

To Bleach Fats

Dissolve a few crystals of potassium permanganate in a pint of soft water. Warm the fat slightly. Add the potassium permanganate solution (1 pint to each pound of fat). Stir occasionally. Add more of the solution if necessary to get a good bleach. Cool and remove the bleached fat.

Utensils

Assemble the proper utensils before beginning the soapmaking.

1. A large enamel or wooden mixing spoon. If wooden, keep it expressly for soapmaking. A smooth stick or an unpainted wooden broom handle sawed to the proper length may be substituted.
2. A stone jar is an excellent vessel in which to mix the lye-and-water solution. Porcelain or enamel can also be used. For larger batches, an iron kettle works well. Never use aluminum utensils (lye acts upon them).
3. A kettle large enough to hold the melted grease.
4. A shallow wooden or cardboard box or metal pan. Cotton cloth to line the box.

Water

Softened or rain water is best for soapmaking. Water may be softened with any of the commercial water softeners or with washing soda.

If hard water is used, the soap may not harden or

may be greasy. This is because part of the lye has combined with some of the hard elements of the water, leaving an insufficient amount of lye to unite with the grease.

Standard Soap Recipe

1 can lye
2½ pints (5 cups) cold water
6 pounds of clear fat
(6¾ pints or 13½ standard
cups of liquid fat)

Use all tallow or a combination of tallow and lard. Add the lye slowly to the cold water. Avert your face while stirring to avoid inhaling fumes. Stir slowly to prevent spattering. Read caution on the lye can.

The solution will become very hot. Allow it to cool until the bottom of the vessel feels lukewarm to the touch. If you are not sure what lukewarm feels like, use a thermometer, which assures success. If you do not have a candy or meat thermometer of the dairy floating type, consult the temperature chart on page 24 for correct temperature of fat and lye.

Melt the fat to a clear liquid and let cool gradually to the correct temperature.

Pour the fat into the lye mixture in a thin, steady stream, with slow, even stirring. Rapid addition or hard stirring may cause a separation.

The soap is ready to pour when it has thickened to a honey-like consistency. Depending upon the size of the batch, it will take from ten to thirty minutes of constant stirring. Another method of judging when to pour it is when the stick stands upright in the soap mixture.

Pour the soap into a wooden box that has been soaked in water and lined with clean cotton cloth dipped in water and wrung nearly dry. The cloth should be long enough to hang over the ends. Smooth the cloth into the bottom.

A cardboard box may be used but do not soak it. With luck you may find a corrugated box with a plastic lining which may be used over and over.

Cover the box of soap with a clean board and an old carpet or other heavy material. Allow it to stand overnight, when it should be firm enough to cut into bars. Lift the soap from the box by the overhanging cloth ends.

Place the soap to dry where air can reach it, but avoid drafts and cold. It should not be allowed to freeze during the first two weeks. It is a good idea to pile it brick fashion to allow air to circulate around it.

In the basic recipe, ammonia and kerosene are not included. Authorities on soapmaking have this to say, "Ammonia, kerosene, carbolic acid, etc., when added to soap, help it little, if any, as the lye usually neutralizes them. They increase the cost and may make the soap harsh on the skin." They do suggest that, "Borax quickens the action of soap."

However, if you wish to add any or all of the ingredients Grandmother considered necessary for good cleansing action, use the following measurements for the standard recipe given above:

> 2 tablespoons borax
> ⅓ to ½ cup ammonia
> ⅓ to ½ cup kerosene
> ⅓ cup sugar (makes a clearer soap)

Causes of Imperfections and Variations in Soap

1. A greasy layer on top of soap indicates that too little lye was used for the amount of fat.
2. Streaked soap shows that the fat and lye solution were not thoroughly mixed.
3. Cracks in the soap may be due to too much stirring or too much free lye; or drying too quickly.
4. A white deposit on the soap may be due to the use of hard water in making the lye solution; a little free lye; or the addition of too much borax.
5. If too cold or too hot temperature is used, or if soap is too vigorously or not thoroughly mixed, a separation may occur. A separation may also result from using exceedingly rancid fat or fat containing salt. Greasy soap forms on top while liquid settles to the bottom.

Reclaiming Soap

There need never be a failure in soapmaking. If separation occurs it can be reclaimed by boiling.

Cut or shave the soap into a kettle, add the lye that has separated out (never throw it away) and about five pints of water. Melt with gentle heat and stir occasionally. Then raise the heat and boil gently. It should become thick and syrupy. If it does not, add more water, one pint at a time, and continue boiling until it becomes ropy or hairy when dropped from a spoon. Pour into mold and cover.

NOTE: Do not be afraid of adding too much water since it can be boiled off.

Tests of a Good Soap

Good soap should have a firm, even texture, neither too moist nor too dry. It will not feel greasy to the hands. It will form smooth curls when shaved.

A neutral soap is practically tasteless and will not "bite" the tongue or smart the skin.

TEMPERATURE CHART

Types of Fat	Temperature of Fats	Temperature of Lye Solution
Sweet rancid fat	97° F. to 100° F.	75° F. to 80° F.
Sweet lard or other soft fats	80° F. to 85° F.	70° F. to 75° F.
Half lard and half tallow	100° F. to 110° F.	80° F. to 85° F.
All tallow	120° F. to 130° F.	90° F. to 95° F.

In hot weather or in a hot room if the soap mixture remains greasy, set it in a pan of cold water and continue stirring until thick, when it is ready to pour. If temperatures are too low, lumps of soap will form and separation will occur. In that case, set the mixture in a pan of warm water and stir gently until it is of the right consistency and all the lye is reincorporated.

NOTE: Avoid hardening of the mixture on the sides and bottom of the pan.

3. Toilet Soap

Making soap in the kitchen sink with an egg beater and a bowl for equipment is a new concept in soapmaking. It is possible for anyone, no matter how limited the space, to become a soapmaker. An evening spent in the kitchen will produce more Christmas presents for less money than nearly any other project in which you could engage.

You can make for pennies soap that would cost dollars in a boutique shop. There you will find soap made from goats' milk, sea mud, beeswax and honey, practically every member of the fruit family, and even a few vegetables and herbs. They sell for as much as $5.00 a bar.

The soaps in the recipes that follow cost from $.14 a bar to $.40 for the extra superfatted imitation castile soap. You will feel like a magician when you turn a few simple ingredients into freshly fragrant fine toilet soap. Making a product that is a daily necessity while knowing that it is free from harmful chemicals, full of natural oils and gentle to the skin provides both a joyful and satisfying experience and a lasting benefit.

To make the best quality toilet soap one must use pure fat (no reclaimed grease) and fresh pure oils. The tallow should be creamy white with fine membranes running throughout. Any blood-stained or otherwise discolored pieces must be removed if you expect to make a pure white soap of good quality.

Cut the tallow into small chunks, the smaller the pieces the faster the tallow will render. It should be melted over low heat to prevent discoloration. An exhaust fan over the stove or a window left slightly open will carry off the odor of melting tallow. A fair amount of tallow can be rendered in an hour so render as much as you expect to use and the greasy kettle will have to be washed only once. It is wise to have the tallow rendered before the day of soapmaking. Stir the tallow occasionally. When most of the fat has been extracted it is ready to strain through several thicknesses of cheesecloth into a bowl. When cold refrigerate. It will keep for several weeks.

The basic ingredients for making toilet soap are the same as for making all-purpose soap, the difference being the oils and other additives such as scents and colors used to enrich and beautify the toilet soap. The possibilities for changing the basic recipe are endless when fat from tallow is combined with any of the following additives. It is up to you to discover the combinations that please you most.

Oils act as superfatting agents. They must be combined with tallow to produce a hard soap. The degree of hardness depends upon the amount of tallow. Oils available in supermarkets are cheaper than those sold in health food stores. The following is a partial list of oils: coconut, olive, castor, sesame, peanut, walnut, corn, sunflower, avocado and apricot kernel oil.

Other beneficial additives are: lanolin, glycerine, Vaseline, cold cream, cocoa butter, bran, almond meal, oatmeal, hand lotions, beeswax, lemon and cucumber juice.

Lanolin is an oil extracted from raw sheeps' wool. It penetrates the skin with ease and is slightly antiseptic. It must be melted in a double boiler. It is sold in drugstores by the ounce.

Cocoa butter is pure fat extracted from the cocoa bean. It is an excellent superfatting ingredient. It must also be melted in a double boiler.

Coconut oil is obtained from the dried meat of coconuts. Today most of the commercial soaps are made from a combination of coconut oil and tallow. It is valued for its free lathering qualities.

Bran, oatmeal and almond meal are mild abrasives. Glycerine, Vaseline, cold cream, hand lotions, and beeswax are enriching agents. Lemon and cucumber juice act as mild astringents.

The basic one-bar soap recipe makes one large bar of all-purpose soap without the additives or four average-size bars of toilet soap with additives. It may be an advantage and a saving to make half batches while experimenting with additives.

Basic One-Bar Soap Recipe

½ cup cold, soft water
2 heaping tablespoons lye
1 cup melted tallow
coloring and scent if desired

Cover the counter area with several thicknesses of newspaper. Place newspapers in the sink if you plan to stir the lye there and don't forget the floor. During the making of over seventy batches of soap I didn't spatter any lye, but I had the misfortune to drop melted candle coloring on the counter. It could not be removed. Thereafter I covered all work areas.

Have a cup of rendered tallow melted and hot, scent measured, and coloring ready to use (see Chapter 4). Have equipment handy: stirring stick, egg beater, measuring spoon, and a glass measuring cup with a lip.

Fill a one-cup measure with melted fat. Before measuring the lye read the label on the can. Lye is more dangerous in its inert dry form than it is after it is mixed with water, but it does attract water. A speck on the hand will mix with perspiration and cause a deep and painful burn. Even in solution it requires careful handling. If you should get lye on your skin run cold water over the spot or rinse with lemon juice or vinegar. Do be careful when using lye around children.

If you should open a partially used can of lye and find the particles stuck together discard the can. The lye has lost some of its strength by absorbing moisture. Avert your head or use an exhaust fan to avoid breathing the lye fumes.

In a bowl with a lip, pour ½ cup of cold soft water. Add to this 2 heaping tablespoons of lye. With a clean stick keep the mixture in motion. The lye will dissolve. If for some reason you are prevented from stirring at the moment and the lye hardens, break up the particles and stir until they dissolve.

The lye-and-water mixture will become very hot. When both the fat and the lye mixtures feel lukewarm to the hand placed on the bottom of the containers, they are ready to combine. A thermometer is really unnecessary when making these small batches since the bowls are small enough to lift easily to test the degree of heat. A little testing and you will be able to determine the lukewarm stage easily. If the lye cools faster than the fat, place a spoon in the cup; it conducts heat away from the fat. Place the cup in a bowl of cold water. If the fat is too cool, place it in a bowl of hot water.

When both mixtures are lukewarm pour the melted fat in a thin, steady stream into the lye and water while stirring slowly and steadily (too rapid pouring and stirring may cause separation). When the last of the fat has been poured add coloring, borax, scent, and any other additive stirring the while.

Remove the stick and beat the mixture with a steady, not too fast, motion until it becomes slightly thickened to the consistency of unbeaten whipping cream. You can use either an old-fashioned hand mixer or a portable electric mixer [1]. It is very much like beating fudge. One minute it is shiny and fluid; the next thing you know it has turned opaque and solid. By lifting the beater from the bowl to observe how much the mixture coats the blades and by noting the resistance to the turning blades you will soon become an expert at telling the proper time to pour the soap into molds. It would take all of the guesswork out of soapmaking if a definite beating time could be established. But this would make the project humdrum and not at all exciting. At any rate, it is not possible since some additives cause soap to "set up" faster than others and the temperature of the ingredients may vary causing a change in the beating time.

However, should you overbeat and suddenly find the

[1]

soap congealed beyond the pouring stage do not despair. You have two choices: The batch can be made into soap balls or the bowl can be placed in a pan of very hot water and the soap stirred until it reaches a pourable stage. It seldom works to pat congealed soap into molds. Bubbles are bound to be trapped in the soap spoiling the quality, and creases generally occur on the outside surface marring the appearance.

It is not wise at this stage to handle soap with the

bare hands. The chemical force that causes lye to act upon the fatty acids has not been completed, the lye is not spent. It is still decidedly caustic. Wear rubber gloves for protection. You can hand form the balls or place a dollop of soap onto a square of plastic wrap. Never place soap on aluminum foil, it blackens at the point of contact. The print of newspapers will also darken soap and wax paper leaves a white film on the surface. After the dollops have stood long enough to set bring the sides of the plastic wrap up around the soap. Twist to tighten the wrap. Remove the plastic, place the soap on glass or plastic and pat out the irregularities with your glove-protected hand or use a spoon. Turn the balls several times to prevent the bottoms from flattening. When they have become firm dip a finger in water and rub them smooth.

These balls can be speared with toothpicks and

[2]

dipped in liquid soap of another color just before the soap is ready to pour. They will become as smooth as silk and look good enough to eat. To dry, stick the toothpicks into styrofoam or Permoplast blocks [2].

There are other soap shapes that you may wish to form by hand rather than cast. The cucumber and strawberries [3] were hand shaped.

To make the cucumber, light green soap was worked into an elongated shape on a piece of glass with a knife blade. When set it was molded by hands protected with rubber gloves. When the soap was firm toothpicks were speared into the bottom near the ends. With the toothpicks as hand holds, the cucumber was immersed in a batch of dark green soap of pouring consistency.

[3]

Several quick dunkings completely covered the light green cucumber. Warts of dark green soap softened over hot water were dripped onto the surface.

The strawberries were started as balls which were drawn out to pointed ends as the balls became set enough to hold their shapes. When the strawberries were firm a blunt pen handle was used to make indentations over the surface. The leaves were cut from stiff paper which was dipped in melted green crayon. A half inch of the stem of a green plastic flower (a section of toothpick painted green could be substituted) was pushed through a hole made in the center of the leaf. The stem was inserted into the strawberry top, leaving a bit of stem protruding. Plastic strawberry leaves can also be purchased. (See Some Sources of Supplies.)

We have learned how to make the basic one-bar recipe which can be used either for the hands or for washing clothes. This recipe will, by the addition of superfatting ingredients, produce the fine toilet soap mentioned earlier. The following recipes are merely suggestions to stimulate your imagination. They have been tried, and each produced a fine soap. Some are richer than others; some encourage more foaming; each combination has its own characteristics.

Explore until you discover just the right soap for you. It should be fast foaming, good smelling, creamy, and mild. Above all it should cleanse efficiently without removing excess amounts of the protective coating on the skin known as sebum. For the most part the ingredients in these recipes are found in the kitchen or bathroom. Most of the oils are found in supermarkets. Cocoa butter, coconut oil, lanolin, and glycerine come from the drugstore.

There are soaps on the market boasting of such additives as wheat germ oil, vitamin E, and protein oil. There is a question whether these additives warrant the extra cost they add to soap, based on the statement of the American Medical Association in an article called "The Look You Like" in *Today's Health.* "It is hardly likely that a good cleansing agent such as soap can accomplish two diametrically opposed tasks in a single washing operation: (1) the removal of soils from the skin and (2) the deposition of fat or cream on the skin."

Each of the following recipes—with the exception of the recipe for Imitation Castile Soap—requires:

> 2 heaping tablespoons of lye added to
> ½ cup cold, soft water

Follow the directions used for mixing the basic one-cup recipe. Pour the superfatting ingredients in a one-cup measure. Add hot melted tallow to fill the cup.

> 1 tablespoon olive oil
> 1 tablespoon peanut oil
> tallow

---

1 tablespoon safflower oil
1–1½ tablespoons olive oil
tallow

---

1 tablespoon olive oil
1 tablespoon safflower oil
1 tablespoon coconut oil

---

1 tablespoon Vaseline or Vaseline lotion
1 tablespoon moisture cream
tallow

The moisture cream will not mix with
the tallow and Vaseline but incorporates
when added to the lye and water.

---

1 tablespoon olive oil
1 tablespoon coconut oil
1 tablespoon glycerine
tallow

½ of one ounce cake of cocoa butter
1 tablespoon olive oil
1 tablespoon castor oil
tallow

¼ cup safflower oil
1 tablespoon lanolin
1 teaspoon borax dissolved in
1 teaspoon soft water
tallow

---

1 tablespoon castor oil
1 tablespoon lanolin
1 tablespoon coconut oil
1 teaspoon borax dissolved in
1 teaspoon of soft water
tallow

Cucumber Soap

1 tablespoon olive oil
1 tablespoon safflower oil
1 heaping teaspoon of whole cucumber
   mixed in a blender to a thick mush
tallow

The procedure for making this soap is the same as for the other recipes with one exception. Mix the cucumber pulp with one tablespoon of dissolved lye from the lye and water mixture. This is necessary to make the cucumber incorporate with the other ingredients.

Castile soap gets its name from Castilla, the region in Spain where it was first produced. Olive oil was plentiful and when combined with tallow it produced a soap of superior quality. Though soap continues to be made in Spain it is seldom made of olive oil because of the cost.

A very high-grade soap, which in many respects is superior to castile soap, can be made as follows:

> ¾ cup olive oil
> 1¼ cups tallow
> ¾ cup coconut oil
> ¼ cup of lye added to
> 1 cup cold, soft water

If you are old enough to remember Jap Rose Soap or have been admiring the rainbow-colored translucent soap in shops, you may want to make your own transparent soap. To do so it is necessary to make a batch of glycerine soap from the following recipe:

> ⅓ cup glycerine
> 2 tablespoons coconut oil
> 2 heaping tablespoons lye
> ½ cup cold, soft water
> coloring and scent if desired
>
> Use yellow coloring to make
> imitation Jap Rose Soap.

38

When the soap is ready to pour use several small molds. Remove from the molds the next day. Allow the soap to cure for 3 days, then grate enough on a fine vegetable grater to make 1½ cups. Place the soap in a small pan. Measure 4 ounces of isopropyl alcohol (91 per cent). Add to the soap. Rubbing alcohol will not work. Stir the mixture until all of the soap is moistened. Improvise a double boiler with a slightly larger pan. Do not allow the water to boil over into the soap. The soap mixture will boil rapidly because alcohol has a low boiling point. Stir constantly.

In a very short time the mixture will thread from the spoon and the soap will be reduced to about half of the original amount. When this happens about 80 per cent of the alcohol will have evaporated. A thin skin usually forms over the soap when you stop stirring. It must be broken in order to pour the soap into molds.

This recipe will make several small bars. When you have made a batch and gloated over the transparent beauty you may wish to make more. One recipe for glycerine soap will make several batches of translucent soap.

Now that you have the feel of the process, change the proportions to 2 cups of grated soap and 1 4-ounce bottle of alcohol. The boiling time will be shorter when less alcohol is used, but the results will be the same.

You can use the glycerine soap recipe to make an excellent rich, creamy shampoo. A pint of shampoo can be made from the recipe and still leave enough soap to make several bars.

Glycerine Shampoo

½ cup of liquid glycerine soap poured
     into a bowl when the soap has been
     beaten to the pouring stage
½ cup of warm, soft water added to the soap
2 tablespoons of baby shampoo or use
     your favorite shampoo
2 tablespoons of coconut oil

Beat together until the ingredients
are thoroughly mixed. The recipe makes about
one pint of shampoo the consistency of cold
cream.

If you have oily hair, add 1½ tablespoons of baking
soda dissolved in 1 teaspoon of water.

A tinted shampoo can be made by adding a strong
tea made of herbs.

Brunettes

1 tablespoon sage leaves
1 tablespoon rosemary
1 cup soft water

Boil for 15 minutes. Cool.
Pour into a glass jar and let stand
overnight. Strain. For each tablespoon
of herb tea add one less tablespoon
of water to the shampoo.

Blonds

3 tablespoons camomile
1 cup soft water

Follow directions for making
sage and rosemary tea.

Another pretty bar of soap is made by swirling two soaps of different colors together in a mold. This requires two people, each making a different color. For the best effect, tint one batch a light color and the other a dark color for contrast. A white soap and a color work well. Use any recipe you like. A half batch of each color for a starter will give an average-size bar of swirled soap and some left over for balls or small molds.

The soap should be thick enough so it can be swirled together without losing the pattern but not so thick that it will set up before you are finished swirling. By drawing an orangewood stick or pencil through the soap additional pattern is produced.

□

4. Perfume and Coloring

Throughout the ages various scents have been in favor and had long and lasting vogue. Today is no exception. Recently the *Wall Street Journal* carried this front-page, full-length column headed, "A Nation Goes Wild Over New Perfume That Smells Like Uh . . ." The perfume is musk and though it smells, as some people say, like stale sweat socks, it retails for about $5.00 a half ounce. This musk oil has nothing to do with the Asian musk deer. It is made of chemicals. The perfume experts are at a loss to know the cause for this sudden craze for musk. Perhaps it is because musk is touted as exotic and erotic or because it is powerful and new. For years it had been the same old thing—lilac, rose, and jasmine. "Musk is strong and it will last for days," said one of its biggest manufacturers. "It doesn't wash off when you swim or bathe." Pure musk is so strong that a piece the size of the head of a pin will scent a room for weeks. It can transfer its odor to almost any other substance, even polished steel. Before the present craze for the scent it was used to combine with other scents to make them permanent.

Lemon is another scent that has been riding the crest of national popularity for the past two years. Its light, crisp, fresh odor is the direct antithesis of the powerful musk. It is artificially made of thirty to forty chemical components. Barely 2 per cent of its fragrance comes from the real lemon, the bulk comes from a plant called lemongrass, grown in the West Indies. Olfaction experts believe the lemon fad stems from the strong interest in nature and naturalism, especially among our college-age people.

Continual testing and experimenting goes on among the large perfume manufacturers in an effort to produce the next odor to become the rage of a capricious public. One expert predicts the "start of a whole new era of animal fragrances." Next on his list: essence of civet and ambergris. If this prediction comes true, the scents will, without doubt, also be chemically produced. Animal scents are principally musk, civet, ambergris, and castor. Because of their lasting qualities, these scents have until now been used as fixatives for other perfumes. They may now become separate scents as has musk.

Real musk is a secretion from the male musk deer. It is a greasy substance produced in a glandular sac beneath the skin of the stomach. It is vile smelling until dried and cured into powder. This musk powder is more expensive than gold. It sells for about $4,000 a pound—more than five times the price of gold. A similar substance is secreted by the musk ox, muskrat, and Florida alligator.

Civet is a secretion of the civet cat. The principal source of supply is Africa, where the civet is kept in confinement. The secretion is removed from a sac near the genital organs twice a week by means of a small spatula.

Castor, the scent from the beaver, has a very pleasant odor when cured and diluted. It is incorporated with other scents to produce combinations that are impossible to obtain in any other manner.

Ambergris is formed within the intestinal tract of the sperm whale and is one of the most valuable of all substances. It is thought to be produced by a diseased condition of the intestines. Some ambergris has been secured from the intestines of sperm whales, but practically all has been found cast up on the beach or floating on the surface of the water.

Vegetable scents may be divided into general classes: those that are resins and those that are oils. Oils are divided into true oils and essential oils. True oils are greasy, lighter than water, and do not evaporate. It is the essential or volatile oils that evaporate without leaving a greasy mark. They are the ones used in perfume making.

Essential oils are found in flower petals, as in the rose and violet; in leaves and stems, as in geranium, sage, and thyme; in wood, as in cedar and sandalwood; in seeds, as in almond and nutmeg; in roots, as in sassafras and orris; in fruit rinds, as in orange, lemon, and lime; in gums, as in camphor, myrrh, and balsam. The odoriferous materials are separated from the plant by distillation, expression, or extraction. It is safe to say that no perfume offered to the public today is made entirely from natural flower extracts. When flower perfumes have been analyzed it is a relatively simple matter to prepare an imitation. Hundreds of perfumes are artificially prepared from chemical compositions that resemble natural perfumes in their odor. Many synthetics, however, do not exist in nature but are the result of chemical research. An example is the ionone having the odor of violets. If perfume makers were forced to rely upon natural violet scent, it would be so expensive only the very rich could afford it, for an acre of the finest violets yields only a few drops of the violet essence.

There are at least 5,000 different scents used throughout the world today, with Americans using far more than any other people. In addition to its use on the person, our weekly wash is delivered scented, we spray our rooms with scent. Stationery, paint, cigarettes, and toilet paper are also scented. There are many scents available in arts and craft catalogues, department stores, apothecary shops, health food stores, hobby shops, and boutiques. Any shop that sells candlemaking supplies sells scents. Prescription drugstores have some essential oils, mainly the aromatic types such as cinnamon, clove, and sassafras. Some of the better scents have the words, "essential oil" printed on the label of the half-ounce bottles. The cost ranges from $.50 to $1.25 or more.

Two don'ts: Never use colognes or toilet water in soap: they contain alcohol and may cause a separation of the soap ingredients. Do not buy candle scents put up in blocks of wax—they are decidedly weaker than the oils.

Because of the present enthusiasm for candlemaking there are many scents available; among them pine, incense, sandalwood, jasmine, redwood, frangipani, lavender, myrrh, lilac, gardenia, oriental bouquet, patchouli, Christmas night, hyacinth, honeysuckle, and the popular musk. Among the fruit scents are strawberry, raspberry, lemon, cherry, watermelon, lime, and tangerine. Experiment to discover which scents or combination of scents remain permanent in soap. Some last longer than others. The aromatic types such as cinnamon, sassafras, and clove are the strongest and an excellent choice for men's soap. However, cinnamon and clove may darken the soap and are best used in a colored soap.

Some scents are very delicate and need the addition of other odors to bring out their character. Lavender is entirely without value when used alone in toilet soap. Patchouli is a heavier oil and one that might be combined with lavender.

Some manufacturers print on the label the amount of candle wax that the bottle of scent will perfume. This cannot be used as a gauge in soapmaking. Because of the nature of soap more scent is required. Generally, a teaspoon or more is needed for the basic one-bar recipe. To get the proper amount you must experiment. While you want a lasting scent in soap, it should not be overpowering. Our sense of smell is probably more refined than that of the Emperor Nero who had the walls of his dining room lined with movable ivory plates concealing silver pipes that sprayed streams of highly odorous perfume on the guests. Experiment until you arrive at a scent that pleases you. Test your perfume by sniffing the contents of the bottle after the oils are thoroughly blended or by dipping a narrow strip of absorbent paper into the bottle and waving it about in the air or by placing a dab on the skin. Keep a record of your formula as you go along so you will be able to reproduce it.

To compound pleasing odors you must blend scents as an artist blends colors. Some produce discord, some harmony. Part of the fun of creating a scent is choosing a name for it, which can also be given to the soap. If the soap is to be a gift, try matching personalities.

When naming scents consider such names as Irresistible, Bold, Naughty, or Shy. Be romantic with Tender Love, Oriental Night, or Mystic Delight. You might tuck in a small vial of perfume with the soap.

All soap readily absorbs odors. It can be inexpensively perfumed by placing layers of aromatic leaves between the soap layers with cheesecloth between soap and leaves to prevent discoloration. Mint, wintergreen, lemon verbena, and rose geranium leaves are especially good for the purpose.

Perfumes go hand in hand with romance. The stories of some of the perfumes are so intriguing you may want to include a brief history of the scent used with a gift of soap. Frangipani, for instance, was a new scent introduced into France in the fifteenth century. A descendant of the Frangipani family of Italy was a marshal in the army of Louis XIII. He wore gloves scented with perfume invented by his ancestors. He was persuaded to share the recipe, and it soon became a popular scent in France and England. It was said that the original Frangipani perfume contained every known spice with orris, civet, musk, and other scents. The frangipani made by today's perfumers contains twenty or more ingredients.

Coloring Soap

With the rainbow array of candle coloring available, any color or combination of colors is possible. In addition to the basic red, blue, green, and yellow, you will find, by shopping around, purple, aqua, gold, lime, flamingo, brown, black, burgundy, avocado, vibrant pink, coral gipsy, violet, rust, and chartreuse. Such a variety is sure to quicken the creative urge of any soap-maker.

Soap can be made to match the decor of a bathroom. Any color can be duplicated by mixing candle colors. Shave a small amount of color into a teaspoon or two of melted tallow. A long-handled coffee measure or a ¼-cup metal measure is a useful piece of equipment for this purpose. Melt over low heat. Excessive heat will change or destroy color. Mix thoroughly, then set the pan into a dish of hot water to keep the mixture liquefied until time to pour it into the soap. The soap will be darker in the liquid stage than when it is dry. To correct this, either add more color or start with a darker color.

Interesting shades may be made by mixing two or more colors, such as blue and green to produce a peacock blue, or various shades of purple by mixing red and blue. To test a color before using it, dip a small piece of paper into the coloring.

Wax crayons, which also come in many colors, can be used to color soap. Crayon does not melt as quickly as candle coloring. To keep it in the liquid stage ready to add to the soap, place the container with the crayon on a very low flame. Wax crayons may be melted with a little tallow to thin them.

Lipstick shaved into tallow can be used when a red or pink color is desired. Cake coloring is not a dependable method of coloring soap. Most colors become a drab gray. Yellow is the most dependable of the colors.

Try correlating the color of the scent with the soap color; violet scent with violet color; pine with green; rose-colored soap with rose scent; and use the proper fruit scent and coloring together.

If two people are making soap, it is possible to combine two colors for a rainbow effect.

Soap sets up rapidly when it has been beaten until it is the consistency of unbeaten whipping cream. To allow the time it takes to pour two colors of soap and swirl them together, the beating time must be cut to about half the regular time it takes for the soap to set up. In order to do this, use a recipe you have used before; one with the approximate thickening time established.

After the first color is poured but not set, add the second color and swirl together with a pencil or orangewood stick. Use colors that combine well, such as yellow and blue, which will produce green where they mix, and blue and pink which give the added color lavender.

5. Special-purpose Soap

In addition to all-purpose soap and toilet soap, many other kinds of useful soap can be made in the home. A thrifty housewife can eliminate all soap and cleanser purchases. There are soaps to fill any need, from removing paint and grease from mechanic's hands to repelling insects and soothing tired feet. The following are a few of the possible special-purpose soaps you can make. With these as guides, experiment with making soaps to fit your particular needs.

Cottonseed Oil Soap

1 can lye
3 pints cold, soft water
5¾ pounds cottonseed oil

Pour lye into water and stir until dissolved. Combine the lye solution and oil when both have reached 135° F.

Follow directions for making standard soap recipe on page 21. The resulting product will be a rather soft soap. For harder soap, substitute tallow for part of the cottonseed oil.

Abrasive Soap

Use the recipe for making the standard batch of soap on page 21. When the mixture thickens add, gradually, 5 to 6 pounds of pumice stone, emery dust, or Tripoli powder and stir until the mixture is thoroughly blended or all of the lye incorporated. Pour into mold and cover. Yield: 14 to 15 pounds.

Abrasive Soap Paste (1)

A fine soap for household scouring and for mechanics' hands. Shave 3 pounds homemade soap and melt it in 3 pints of water. Add 3 ounces of light mineral oil. When this is thoroughly blended, allow it to cool to a thick consistency and work in 5 pounds of pumice stone or Tripoli powder. Keep tightly covered to prevent drying out of paste. Yield: 11 pounds.

Abrasive Soap Paste (2)

One pound of homemade soap cut or shaved into small pieces; 1 pint hot water; 2 ounces of mineral oil; 1 pound of powdered pumice stone. Melt the soap in hot water; add mineral oil and mix well. When mixture has cooled add pumice stone. Store in tightly covered glass jars to prevent drying. Variation: In addition to the above, add 2 ounces of turpentine and 1 pint of fine sawdust, omitting ⅓ of the pumice.

Jelly Soap

For use in washing machines and for washing dishes. Lye hard soap converted into jelly soap is convenient and economical to use. Cut 1 pound of hard soap into fine shavings and add 1 gallon of water. Boil for about 10 minutes, then transfer to a suitable vessel to cool. Keep covered to prevent drying out. Jelly soap melts in hot water immediately and makes thick suds.

Soft Soap

The following recipe will produce good-quality soft soap.

Dissolve 2 ounces of lye in 3 cups of cold soft water. Pour this into 1 pound of melted tallow. Heat and stir to mix thoroughly. Let cool. When cool if the soap is too firm a jelly, add more water and reheat.

Liquid Soap

Cottonseed oil, 4 pounds; coconut oil, 1¼ pounds; glycerine, 3 pints; alcohol, 6½ pints; water, 7 pints. Dissolve 1 can of lye in a mixture of 3½ pints each of alcohol and water and heat to 125° F. Have the oils at 150° F. and add a few ounces of the lye solution, stirring slowly and evenly. When saponification is about complete, add a few ounces of lye solution stirring constantly and repeat until all the lye solution is in. Cottonseed oil is sometimes rather hard to saponify, and slight separation of oil might occur if the lye has been added too rapidly. In this case, allow it to stand 24 to 48 hours with occasional stirring. When a perfect mixture is obtained with no separation of oil, add the glycerine and the remaining alcohol and water. Allow to stand for a couple of days and if any sediment settles out, filter or syphon off the clear liquid. Then color and perfume as desired.

Fish Oil Soap

One can of lye; fish oil, 4½ pounds; water, 3 pints; lye solution, 80° F.; oil, 100° F. Stir well for about 10 minutes and then allow to stand with occasional stirring until combination is complete. Transfer to the molds. This soap is used as a basis for insecticide and fungicide sprays.

Certain scents, such as citronella and pennyroyal, keep off gnats, flies, and mosquitos. But it is interesting to note that other odors, made up of chemical compounds called amines, attract insects. They fly miles to the source, where they are destroyed en masse. Geraniol, a chemical, attracts Japanese beetles. Cats are attracted to catnip in the same way.

Equal amounts of camomile and nettle may be added in soap to repel insects.

Linseed Oil Soap

One can of lye; linseed oil, 5¾ pounds; water, 4 pints; lye solution, 90° F.; oil, 100° F. Add lye solution a little bit at a time and combine well each time before adding more. This makes a soft soap, recommended for washing automobiles and furniture.

Tar Soap

A lard or tallow soap is made in the regular manner and allowed to stand with occasional stirring until it has become quite thick. Eight ounces of wood tar is then added and worked in. Stir and beat the mass thoroughly to prevent small lumps from forming.

Hard White Soap From Cracklings

Combine 2 gallons water and 3 cans of lye. Allow to cool an hour or more. Place on stove and add 15 pounds of fat scraps. Allow to boil until every scrap is dissolved. Add a total of 2 gallons more water, adding only enough at one time to keep the products from boiling over. Set to cool until next day. Skim solid substance from the surface. Place it in clean kettle and boil 2 hours. Add boiling water until soap becomes the consistency of honey when dropped from a stirring stick. If too much is added, boiling will need to be prolonged. Pour into molds. Cover while cooling.

Rosin Soap

Rosin added to soap increases its lathering properties but makes a darker and softer soap. It is frequently used as laundry soap. Add 8 ounces of crushed rosin to 5½ pounds of clean fat and raise the temperature until the rosin is melted or dissolved in the fat. Cool the mixture to 100° F. and add the lye solution made by dissolving 1 can of lye in 2½ pints of water and cooling to 90° F. If soap containing more rosin is desired, for every 8 ounces of rosin added decrease the amount of fat used by 8 ounces. The total weight of rosin and fat should be 6 pounds for each can of lye.

Hard Soap by the Boiling Process

Prepare in usual manner but do not pour into molds. Keep covered and set in a warm place over night. Next day, cut into fine shavings, add 7 pints of water and melt with gentle heat, stirring occasionally. When all lumps are dissolved, raise the heat and continue boiling until mixture is of a syrupy nature when dropped off of the spoon or paddle. Then pour into molds. Boiling process soaps require more aging than cold process soaps. Perfumes, colors, and other special materials are added after the soap has cooled somewhat, but while it is still fluid enough for pouring.

Tallow Soap

One can of lye; mutton or beef tallow, 6 pounds; water, 2¾ pints; lye solution, 90° F.; fat, 130° F. Soap made with tallow as the only fat is often referred to as "saddle soap" because it is valuable as a cleaner and preserver of leather. Substitution of 1 pound of tallow with lard, coconut, or olive oil will improve the lathering properties.

Coconut Oil Soap

One can of lye; coconut oil, 4½ pounds; water, 2½ pints; lye solution, 70° F.; oil, 110° F. This soap gives a very profuse but thin lather. Substitute tallow or lard for part of this oil for thicker lather.

Coconut oil alone yields a hard soap which is too insoluble for use in fresh water. It lathers in salt water, however, and is used as marine soap.

Foot Soap

A soothing foot soap can be made by using either the recipe for all-purpose soap or the one-bar toilet soap recipe and adding any of the following: menthol, camphor, eucalyptol, wintergreen, or oatmeal, which has been used and valued for centuries as a softener.

Floating Soap

Almost any type of soap can be made to float. When the soap mixture is thick enough fold air into it as egg white is folded into a cake mixture.

□

6. Molding Soap

The possibilities for molding soap are endless. Searching for suitable containers becomes a fun thing, with friends joining in the search to gloat with you over each new find. Containers come from the most unlikely places. An interesting plastic form was given to me by a nurse. It had been the packing for a delicate instrument. Look around the house, the kitchen in particular, for sauce dishes, bottle caps, furniture cup casters, and ash trays. Children's toy muffin pans cast pretty, individual-size shapes [4]. Take time to browse through grocery, dime, and department stores and by all means send for gourmet gift catalogues (see Some Sources of Supplies). You will find madeline pans, tiny fluted tart molds, sandbakkelese molds, square cup cake molds, and miniature loaf pans. Don't overlook the marzipan, sucker, candy, and candle molds. They yield a wealth of forms including fruit, flower, vegetable, animal, and special holiday designs. These molds are inexpensive, with the exception of the rubber candy molds which reproduce as many as twenty-five shapes of one kind.

It is not difficult to remove soap from molds if you remember to grease the mold before pouring the soap. Vaseline or vegetable oil will do. Vaseline stays in

[4]

place and will not run down the sides of the mold. Be sure the inside of the mold is completely covered. Bare spots may cause the soap to stick, in which case it will be necessary to pry gently in order to remove the soap. If the soap does not let go after prying, turn it over and give a sharp tap to the bottom of the container. The soap will fall out.

Another reason for failure to get soap out of molds is attempting to remove it before it has dried sufficiently. Allow the soap to dry in the molds overnight or longer. Rainy days seem to slow up the drying process. The soap will shrink and pull away slightly from the mold when it has dried enough.

By removing soap from the mold too soon an outer part that has dried faster than the rest of the soap may break off. Should this happen, it is possible to put the parts together with a bit of soap melted over hot water. The melted soap can also be used to fill in indentations.

If any of the containers you have chosen to use are made of aluminum, they must be sprayed with metal lacquer or plastic spray to prevent the lye in the soap mixture from acting upon the metal causing it to pit and turn black. When this happens the aluminum blackens the soap on contact. Tin should also be protected by a spray since it is discolored by soap.

Using molds that shape and decorate in one operation is the quickest and easiest way of making attractive bars of toilet soap. The plastic [5 and 6]

[5]

dividers used in packaging cookies are such molds. There are several shapes and sizes. Look for them in the cookie section of any store but look sharply, they are transparent and difficult to see under cellophane wrapping. Generally, these dividers are large enough to make a family-size bar, but with luck—especially at Christmas time—small ones can be found that hold bite-size fruit cakes, marzipan, and other holiday goodies. Handle these molds with care, especially when washing them, and they will hold up for repeated pourings.

Then there are the molds found in craft shops and craft catalogues intended for candlemaking, ceramics, papier-mâché, and plaster of Paris ornaments [5].

When these molds are used to make Christmas ornaments insert a hanger made of string, fine wire, or ribbon in the back before the soap sets. To use these molds to cast toilet soap, a wall of Permoplast must be

[6]

built up from the motif to give a practical thickness to the soap. Permoplast is a plastic modeling clay available in hobby and dime stores in one-pound packages in a variety of colors. Yellow works best since the darker colors have a tendency to bleed into the soap. If the dark colors are used, they should be sprayed in the same way the aluminum was sprayed.

Plan for plain bars of soap to be decorated later by making ovals, rounds, squares, and triangles of various sizes.

If you have in mind making shower soap on cords, consider the many plastic bottles available on grocery and cosmetic shelves. The small pear-shaped bottles with short necks work best. Cut the bottle in half. Scissors will do the job unless the plastic is very heavy and brittle, then sawing is the answer. Rejoin the parts and cover the joint with Permoplast to make it water tight. Weatherstripping and calking cord are useful materials for sealing joints. They come in rope form and are slightly more adhesive and softer than Permoplast. They are generally sold in hardware and paint stores. More will follow on making shower soap.

Thus far the containers suggested for soap casting have been either found in the home or purchased, and the soap from these molds would be decorated by designs incorporated in the mold or by decorations applied later.

There is another method of obtaining exciting, professional-looking soap and that is by making your own mold into which you press objects to get raised designs.

Start your search for suitable things to imprint in your costume jewelry box. Surprising designs turn up.

It's a joy to find an especially appropriate motif such as a cameo, a seahorse pin, a bracelet with lovely raised design, a lion head, a medallion, or monogrammed pin [7]. Display racks of zipper ornaments are loaded with excellent imprinting material. If you are looking for appropriate designs for men's soap, look at belt buckles, cuff links, and raised designs on liquor bottles and glasses.

One soapmaker found beautiful raised signs of the zodiac surrounding a barometer on the wall of a doctor's waiting room. She was allowed to make Permoplast molds of the signs. A cluster of grapes was made from an impression of grapes on a wrought-iron porch column. Buttons, especially some of the antique ones,

[7]

drawer knobs, coins, children's blocks with raised letters, and countless other objects are just waiting to be found. If you have access to antique glassware, there is a treasure of design on the bottoms of pressed and cut-glass dishes. The covers on daguerreotype cases are beautifully designed. Pressing them into Permoplast and removing them at once will do them no harm. A small picture frame is one of the most versatile objects to cast. I used one 3¼ inches × 4¼ inches. It is quite ornate, having a beaded rim. A search for a small frame is well worth the effort because of the many ways in which it can be decorated. (See Chapter 7.)

To make a one-piece mold take a wad of Permoplast, the size depending upon the object to be cast, work it in your hands until it is pliable, then roll it flat with a rolling pin. The thickness depends upon the object to be imbedded. Press the object firmly into the flat, smooth surface of the Permoplast, being careful to apply pressure evenly to all areas. Remove by prying gently from all sides before lifting it from the Permoplast. This depression will make a raised design on the soap [8].

There are two simple ways of making a wall for the cast. A ring may be cut from a plastic juice can or detergent bottle. It should be somewhat higher than the intended thickness of the soap. Center the ring carefully over the design and press evenly into the Permoplast far enough to hold it securely but not through the base [9]. The wall can also be made of Permoplast. Roll a flat strip ¼ inch thick and long enough to encompass the base which has been cut to the proper size and shape. The width of the strip should be slightly more than the thickness you intend

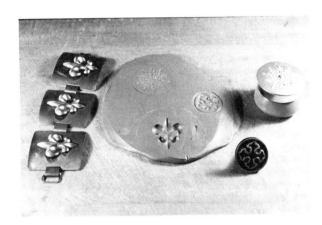

[8]

[9]

to make the soap. Press the wall firmly against the sides of the base. Where the ends join press together and rub out the seam mark with a finger.

Two-piece molds will enable you to cast three dimensional forms. This type of mold is useful in casting vegetables, fruit, or anything you wish to cast in the round. No doubt you have seen the attractive vegetable and fruit soaps in shops. You can make your own mold by modeling the fruit or vegetable in Permoplast, then casting it in plaster of Paris. In some cases the actual fruit can be cast. Firm apples, oranges, lemons and cucumbers cast well. Strawberries must be very green and firm, otherwise they will deteriorate in the casting process.

To successfully cast fruit, fill undercuts with Permoplast and cut away jutting spots in order that the fruit can be lifted from the cast with ease. When this is not done soap cast in the mold will also stick. It is possible to fill these indentations with weatherstrip or to trim the form to eliminate the undercuts. There are commercial fruit and vegetable molds available. The walls of most of them have to be built up.

If you are unable to find the thing you have in mind to cast, do not hesitate to model it of Permoplast. Of necessity these forms must be simple and compact, with a minimum of detail. Feathers, scales, and other designs may be carved on later. The fish shower soap is an oval with the mere suggestion of fins and a short simple tail. If you wish, cut out a form from a child's coloring book or trace around a cookie cutter onto a thick piece of rolled Permoplast, round the edges, and it is ready to cast [10 and 11].

There are several materials from which molds can

[10]

[11]

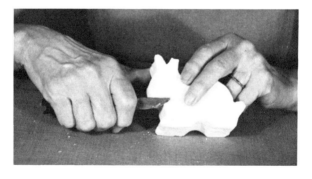

be made. The most common are plaster of Paris, commercial papier-mâché mixes and a mixture of sawdust and wallpaper paste. We will confine ourselves to the use of plaster of Paris since it is cheap, quick, easy to use, and readily available. Should you be interested in trying other casting materials, there are many books on the subject. To make a plaster cast look for a suitable container into which the plaster can be poured. It must be large enough to allow a space of an inch or two around the object to be cast. Any cardboard or plastic box will do. The height can be cut down. Oatmeal and salt boxes and plastic bleach bottles are useful for small casting. Lacking a container, it is easy to make one.

Suppose you are casting a lemon. Cut a strip of bendable cardboard long enough to surround the lemon with the necessary space, plus an additional inch for stapling the ends together. For the height, allow for the thickness of the lemon plus an inch or more at the top and bottom [12]. The box may be

[12]

round, oval, square, rectangular, or any shape that fits
the object best. Bend into shape and staple. Set the
wall onto a heavy piece of cardboard or glass that is
larger than the base of the wall. With Permoplast or
weatherstrip reinforce the outside of the wall where it
and the base come in contact. The wall could also be
made of Permoplast as described on page 71. Before
mixing the plaster draw a line with a felt tipped pen
around the lemon from end to end. This is a pre-
cautionary measure to prevent imbedding more than
half of the lemon and thus making removal impossible.

To mix plaster put as much water in a pan as the
quantity of plaster needed. After making a mold or
two you will be able to judge the amount with some
accuracy. Sift the plaster slowly into the water until a
mound appears on the surface. Stir slowly until it
thickens. Do not lift the spoon from the mixture. This
causes bubbles to form, making holes in the finished
cast. Adding salt will speed the thickening action while
a little vinegar will retard the process.

When the mixture is the consistency of thick cream
pour it into the greased mold or box to a depth that
will allow for imbedding one half of the lemon plus
the wall. Press the lemon into the plaster up to the
half-way mark. If it is a plastic lemon you may have
to hold it down until the plaster is firm enough to
keep it in place. After the plaster has hardened dig
two or three shallow holes about the size of a pencil
eraser into the surface around the lemon. When the
second part of the mold is poured these form a tongue
and groove arrangement which positions one part upon
another.

Before pouring the second half of the cast grease

the mold and the exposed half of the lemon with Vaseline. Mix enough plaster to cover the lemon to a depth of an inch or more. Pour the plaster slowly into the container shaking gently to remove bubbles that may have formed. When the plaster mold is dry remove the cardboard box and pry the two sections apart. If they were properly greased, they will come apart easily.

In order to pour soap into the mold an opening must be made in the cast. The lemon has the opening in the top [13]. Carve a ½-inch hole in the plaster of one section. Place the second half of the cast in position and mark the location for the other half of the hole. Before pouring soap into a plaster mold grease

[13]

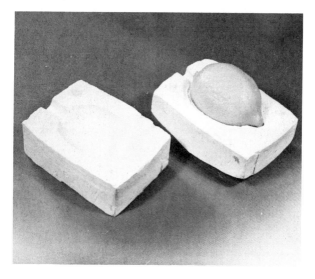

the inside surface of each part with Vaseline. Position one part upon the other, matching tongues to grooves. Bind the sections together with strong rubber bands or string. Seal the joint with Permoplast, and the cast is ready for the soap. Allow soap to set overnight or until it is hard.

If the lemon is to be shower soap buy one yard of cotton cord from a dime or yard-goods store. Bring the ends together and wrap them with string to the depth of one inch. This stiffens the cord and makes it easier to push it into the soap to a depth that will hold it securely. Clamp a clothespin on the cord where it emerges from the cast to hold it upright [14].

[14]

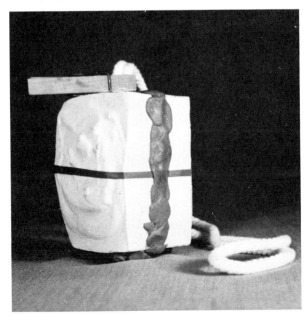

Soap for Children

Children's soap is a perfect stocking stuffer and a joyful gift. Happiness is washing with a cunning bug or jolly Santa as a helper [15]. The sources for molds previously mentioned will yield many suitable designs for children. Popsicles are made in chicken, turkey, reindeer, Santa Claus, and Christmas tree forms. The tiny animals made in marzipan molds can be glued to the tops of plain bars with Goo, an all-purpose, waterproof flexible adhesive [16]. There are gelatin-mold sets of animals and candy molds. Trick-or-treat sandwich

[15]

and cookie cutters can be pressed into Permoplast bases and poured with soap. The resulting form may be left as is or carved into a round form by cutting off the sharp edges. (See page 74.) Molds suitable for children's soap are also available in craft shops where the plastic pumpkin head and Santa Claus molds were purchased.

There are delightful little figures such as trains, animals, and children in decorating sets and among party favors. These may be pressed into Permoplast to make raised designs on the soap. Other simple but effective decorations may be found on greeting cards, gift-wrapping paper, or in magazines. Glued on and sprayed with a plastic spray, they will outlast the soap. Soap figures such as the snowman [16] can be built up

[16]

onto a plain bar by forming two flattened balls of white soap on a colored background. Paint eyes, buttons, mittens, and scarf with melted crayon. The ideas presented here should start you thinking. Give soap that represents a child's special interest or hobby. It may be a football, a pet dog, cat, or parakeet with its special coloring and marking.

Another dimension to children's soap may be added by making ceramic dishes to hold the soap. The dishes shown here were designed with simplicity in mind and can be made without previous work in clay [15].

The soap figures were made and dried before the dishes were formed, with the exception of the Santa, which was made in a commercial two-piece plastic candle mold, and the baseball, cast from a plastic dimestore ball. The forms were molded in Permoplast, then cast in plaster.

The lines on the turtle shell were cut in with an orangewood stick. An interesting effect results when a light green or orange shell is dipped in a darker green and the lines etched through to the under color.

The bug, a simple form consisting of a flattened oval body and round head was made of Permoplast and cast in plaster. When only one is needed it would be easier to make it by hand. It was made of white soap with the colors painted on. The colors used were black, yellow, orange, and white. If you are working with other designs calling for orange soap, try an orange lady bug and paint on the black spots.

The plastic ball was cast in two pieces. The stitching marks showed in the cast. They made raised marks on the soap. These were touched up with light blue melted crayon.

The white soap snail shell was cast in two pieces made necessary by the cut-in design on either side. It, too, could have been made by hand.

The light blue bird was also cast in a two-piece mold. The breast was dipped in white liquid soap; the black eyes and yellow bill were painted on with melted crayon. Feathers were etched in with a wood-working tool.

By allowing the soap figures to dry a week or more a better fit is possible when making the clay dishes.

There are ceramic shops and classes where you can make arrangements to have your work fired and glazed. For best results buy clay where it is to be fired since there are several types with varying firing temperatures. A pound of clay, which costs approximately $.35, will make several dishes. Firing and glazing costs are extra.

By following these simple rules you will have no difficulty in making a ceramic dish.

1. Roll a lump of clay with a rolling pin to a thickness of $3/16$ inch to $1/4$ inch. To get a uniform thickness, place rulers or sticks of the desired thickness on either side of the lump.

2. Whenever possible pinch out parts rather than adding on.

3. When attaching one piece of clay to another, roughen the surfaces to be joined with an orange-wood stick or other pointed object. Apply slip (clay softened in water to a creamy consistency). Press the pieces firmly together. This makes for a good bond and prevents bubbles from being trapped between the pieces. When this happens

the bubbles expand and the piece blows up in the kiln.

4. Clay must be no more than ½ inch thick at any point.
5. Allow clay to dry for two or three weeks before firing.

We will start with the easiest dish to make; the leaf that holds the bug. Pick a real leaf of the right size. It must be large enough to hold the bug and allow for turning up of the sides. It should have a simple outline.

Place the leaf underside down on a piece of rolled clay. Press the leaf into the clay with a rolling pin to make a clear imprint of the leaf and its veins. Remove the leaf and cut out the clay leaf with a pointed knife [17]. Leave a long stem ¼ inch wide if you wish to

[17]

[18]

curl it into a handle. Crimp the edges of the leaf to form the dish sides [18].

Santa's chimney is made of slabs of rolled clay. To get a proper fit, measure him at his widest girth. Cut four side pieces wide enough to hold him upright with a ¾-inch leeway for drying and overlapping of the sides. Make the chimney waist high. Cut a bottom slab that will allow ¼-inch ledge all around. Follow directions for attaching one piece of clay to another. Set the pieces ¼ inch in from the edge of base. Cut a narrow band of clay long enough to encompass the upper edge of the chimney. Attach it to the top by bending it at right angles at each corner. Obliterate the seam joint by moistening a finger and rubbing across the line. When the clay is dry scratch in the brick lines.

To make the snail dish place the soap shell on a piece of rolled clay to determine the size of the snail dish. Allow for a rim and keep in mind that the clay will shrink a little as it dries. Mark out the shape, a long oval, pointed at one end and with a generous circle at the other for the head (if you allow too much, a piece can be removed later), cut around the outline, and wad the circle of clay into a ball, being careful as you do so not to detach it from the body. Shape the ball to a slight point for the nose. Horns may be pinched out from the top of the head or very carefully applied as mentioned above. To keep the clay within the ½-inch tolerance make a hole with a pencil or orangewood stick up into the underside of the head where it will not show. Crimp the edges of the snail to form the sides of the dish. It may be necessary to bolster the sides of the dish with crumpled wax paper to keep them in place until dry enough to hold their shape.

The turtle can be made in the same manner as the snail or it can be made with an applied rim. To do this cut an oval bottom and a rim ¼ inch high and long enough to encircle the base. Attach the rim to the base. In this case the head is made as a separate piece and attached to the rim and base after it has been pierced from the underside to control the thickness. It will need support from underneath while drying. If the head is a part of the whole from the beginning, the rim is attached to the base from one side of the head to the other.

To make the catcher's mitt, a very simple compact shape, form it of Permoplast. A picture of a mitt or the real thing will be a help. Make the size in relation to the ball which should not be too large for small hands. The mitt shown is 3 inches × 5 inches at the widest points. Drape the rolled clay over the model and press into shape leaving a ½-inch to ¾-inch overhang. Turn this edge under to give the impression of thickness. Allow space on the underside in order to remove the Permoplast model when the clay has dried sufficiently to hold its shape. A realistic touch may be added by squeezing segments of clay from a glue bottle with a nozzle. These resemble stitching. They could be painted on the mitt.

To make the bird's nest, you will need a form such as a small round bottomed dish or child's ball. If you are using a ball, anchor it onto a piece of Permoplast to keep it in place. Grease the ball with Vaseline. Drape a piece of dampened cheesecloth over the ball. Smooth it down to avoid creases. Drape a piece of rolled clay over the cloth. Press it tightly against the cloth before you trim it off to form a shallow nest. The cloth that extends below the clay will make removing the nest easy when the clay has dried enough to hold its shape.

While the clay is soft, "twigs" may be applied to the outside of the nest by squeezing nodules of softened clay from a plastic bottle to cover the surface. The clay must be very soft but still hold its shape.

When the nest has dried sufficiently to hold its shape remove it from the ball by lifting the cheesecloth. Place it upon a previously modeled branch with three prongs. This forms a base and support for the nest. Press the nest into place. Make a hole in the bottom on the underside where nest and branch are attached to comply with the ½-inch tolerance.

Leaves and flowers of clay may be added to the branches.

A puppet bath mitt is another stocking stuffer sure to please the small fry. What child could resist a rabbit with perky ears and a mouth to snap open and shut?

The pattern requires almost ½ yard of 36-inch terry cloth, three balls of fringe for the ears and nose, and a small piece of terry cloth of a second color to line the ears and make the mouth. Use a white shoestring or piece of tape for a drawstring. While you are making the rabbit make a mitt for Mama.

You will need powdered soap to fill the mitts. If you have none that you are willing to consign to the grinder, make a batch and pour it into a shallow flat dish. When it is hard break it into pieces. It will cure faster.

Directions for Making Rabbit Puppet Bath Mitt

Cut 3 pieces of pattern No. 1, one mouth laid on a fold, and 4 ear pieces—2 of the puppet color and 2 of the accent or mouth color.

Cut 2 inches from the top of *one* of the 3 pieces of pattern No. 1. This is the back piece. (See sketch of back of mitt.) Hem the top of this piece. Sew ear pieces together, turn right side out, bring lower edges together as shown. Sew in place. Cover ends of ears with balls from fringe and sew on nose.

Sew curved top side of the mouth to curve of the

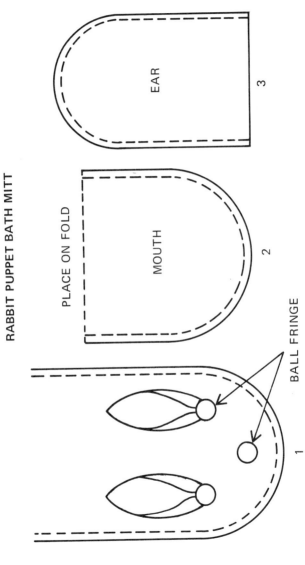

RABBIT PUPPET BATH MITT

EAR 3

PLACE ON FOLD

MOUTH 2

BALL FRINGE

1

Diagram A

face. Sew curved bottom of mouth to third piece of pattern No. 1. The fold of the mouth will be between the two sections. Place the 3 sections together, face turned in. Stitch around outside edge. Turn. Hem top, allowing for drawstring.

Diagram B

BACK OF BATH MITT

□

___

7. Decorating Soap

By giving free rein to your imagination you can turn plain bars of soap into soap so special your guests will hesitate to use it.

This can be done by painting, stamping, incising, stenciling, writing upon it, or by decorating it with paper or plastic designs or decals. It can also be enhanced by cutting shapes from a bar and filling the void with soap of a contrasting color. It can be personalized with photographs.

Paint can be either temporary or permanent. Water colors, tempera, pastels, Craypas, candle colors, and acrylics (unless sprayed with clear plastic) are of a temporary nature. They may be used where a touch of color is desired, but not necessary, as in the case of the angel [19] which would also be charming in just white. For flesh tones, Craypas—a combination of crayon and pastel or water color—may be used, especially on hands and faces, for a realistic touch. For larger surfaces, a combination of melted candle coloring with a little tallow added covers well and is easy to apply. This was used to paint Santa's suit red. Waterproof paint over so much of the surface would have rendered the soap unusable. Soap should be cured

[19]

before using this mixture to prevent bleeding into the surrounding areas.

To achieve a lasting glossy color use melted wax crayon with a little beeswax added to make it less brittle and easier to apply. It must be kept hot but not smoking, and the brush should be held in the mixture to heat it thoroughly before applying the color to the soap. Fast work and frequent dipping is necessary, but the results are worth the effort.

The balls of decorated soap for Christmas [19] were painted with melted crayon applied with heavy short strokes giving them a raised appearance. Shading was done with darker colors, adding to the dimensional look. The dots made for Christmas tree trimming, mistletoe, and holly berries were dripped on from a full brush and are considerably raised. Names and initials can be painted on the soap with melted crayon and a fine-tipped brush. Practice on a piece of paper before tackling the soap, although mistakes can be scraped from the surface and a new start made. Acrylic paint is an easier medium to work with but will wash off unless sprayed with several coats of clear plastic spray [20].

An art melter with a eight-cup palette is a useful appliance for melting crayons or candle coloring and beeswax [21]. It keeps them at the proper temperature and is safer to use than working on a stove burner. (See Some Sources of Supplies.)

Incising or engraving into the soap is a quick and simple method of decoration. It can be done on fresh

[20]

[21]

or cured soap [22]. Lines may be cut into the soap
with an orangewood stick, but a greater variety of ef-
fects is possible with a set of wood-block or linoleum
cutting tools. There are U-shaped, V-shaped, and
gouging tools of varying widths. An all-over pattern on
a flat bar of rectangular soap would be a good place to
start [23]. A simple design consisting of straight or
wavy lines filled in between with interesting gouges
made by the tools mentioned could be done freehand. It may be less than perfect, but the irregularity
of handwork is its chief charm. It can't be duplicated
and it won't look commercially made.

[22]

[23]

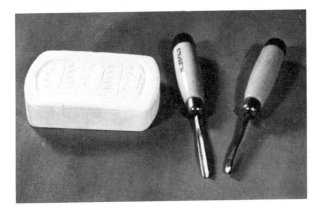

For a more complicated design, draw a pattern on a piece of paper cut the size and shape of the soap. Hold the paper in place on the soap, drawing side up, and trace the lines with a pencil bearing down hard enough so that the lines can be easily seen on the soap. Incising may be combined with painting for a pleasing effect.

Stenciling is another easy method of decorating soap. For this process a simple bird design was cut from a piece of stencil paper. Any heavy paper will do [24]. Cut the paper the size and shape of the soap; it will be easier to center it on the bar. Cut out the center of the design with a small scissors or a replaceable-blade utility knife. (See Some Sources of Supplies.) Before positioning the stencil on the soap wipe the underside with a thin film of Vaseline. This will hold it in place

[24]

and prevent spray or paint from seeping under the edges of the stencil. This makes for sharper lines and is especially necessary on rounded bars of soap. The opening in the stencil may be sprayed or painted with gold paint or painted with acrylic paint. Several coats may be necessary if you are using gold paint. When paint is dry protect the design with several coats of clear plastic spray.

Decorating with applied paper designs will be a favorite method of decoration for anyone who wishes to achieve a pleasing effect with a minimum of effort. There are many sources of suitable motifs. Greeting cards, wrapping paper, wallpaper, bridge tallies, contact paper, playing cards, decoupage materials, paper doilies, stationery, and decals offer endless possibilities for the adornment of soap. Greeting cards are the most fertile field because of the many occasions they cover. Anything from the simplest flower to the most elegant dimensional crest may be found together with beautifully embossed lettering in gold, silver, and colors. Some of the most noteworthy designs come from Mother's and Father's Day cards. It is here that you are most apt to find suitable designs to apply to soap for men. You can cater to special interests such as hunting, fishing, or golfing.

The old stand-by, the decal, should not be overlooked [25]. There are handsome and colorful designs available on many subjects. They will remain intact until the soap is used up.

Embossed braids and trims used in the art of decoupage come in handy as borders and accents. The larger medallions can be cut apart to obtain different-size decorations. The one shown [26] was done on soap

[25]

[26]

cast in the form of a picture frame. A medallion was used to frame a cutout from a colored photograph. The medallions were also used in two other photograph cutouts.

Using photographs provides an opportunity to give an extra personal touch to your gift—a cat belonging to a friend, flowers from another's garden, a snapshot of a friend. A doting grandmother would be pleased with a picture of a favorite grandchild or a friend caught in a humorous situation would be good for a laugh.

The photographs and their frames are attached to the soap with glue. All paper decorations, other than decals, should be glued to the soap with either Sobo glue or Goo, then given several coats of clear plastic.

Plastic cameos from a craft shop provides decoration for several bars of soap. They are available in black or white and in several sizes. Plastic trim pins make colorful accents. They come in assorted colors but must be broken off since they are an inch long. To make sure they will stay in the soap push them in, remove them and apply a bit of glue to the tips before reinserting them into the soap.

The two remaining methods of soap decoration to be discussed, imprinting an object into the surface of the soap and one in which a design is dug out of the soap and then filled with soap of another color, must be done before the soap is cured.

To stamp a perfect design onto a bar of soap, the soap must be of the right consistency, neither too soft nor too hard. After the soap has been poured test it frequently. If it is greasy on top the object will slide and blur the design. If it is too hard the imprint will be shallow and there is a possibility of chipping the soap. A little practice will give you the know-how to make a perfect print. It is always possible to shave off the top and decorate the bar in another manner.

I have used an antique daguerreotype case and a Sandwich glass cup plate to print soap. The bottoms of many pieces of glassware have attractive designs. The best prints result from impressions made from objects with raised instead of depressed designs [27].

The cutting away process of decoration is most successfully done when the soap is fresh but firm. Hard, cured soap would have a tendency to chip as the cutter or knife is removed. Also, the freshly poured

[27]

soap might shrink and pull away from the sides of the cured soap. If a cookie cutter is being used to make the design, press it into the soap, the depth depending upon the thickness of the soap. Slowly, carefully, withdraw the cutter. With a penknife or razor blade dig the soap away from the inside of the design, being careful to preserve a sharp clean line [28].

Fill the indentation with fresh colored soap. Where color separation is necessary, such as between flower and leaves, a small piece of cardboard or a bit of Permoplast can be used to make a temporary wall. When the first color is set remove the wall and pour the second color.

[28]

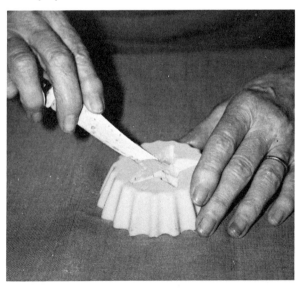

8. Packaging Soap

For a final touch, package the soap you have made. It deserves the best setting you can give it. This isn't difficult with the great variety of materials and containers from which to choose. There are many things never intended to hold soap that do it beautifully with very little work on your part.

The long plastic and cardboard trays in which cookies and other foods are packaged, real shells, odd cups and saucers, bath-powder boxes, small baskets, rattan cracker trays, and small wicker cornucopias, to name but a few, will require no more than plastic wrap, a bow, and a sprig of flowers [29 and 30].

There are boxes that need a little help on your part to make them attractive, such as the pharmacists' hinged cardboard pillboxes, candy and cigar boxes, plastic detergent bottles, and the many boxes made of tin. Wooden berry boxes are appropriate containers for fruit and vegetable soap when cut down to one or two inches. Those with wooden rims are easiest to convert. Remove the staples holding the rim, cut the box to the desired height with scissors, and restaple the rim to the box. Boxes with metal rims can be resized but require more time.

Small-appliance cases are one of the best sources of

[29]

[30]

well-made hinged boxes. Look for razor, watch, and jewelers' boxes. Cosmetic containers are generally attractive and are often oval or round.

You can, of course, hie yourself to a shop for a ready-made soap dish. The dime store offers simple plastic dishes, hinged boxes, and copies of more expensive soap dishes. You can splurge in a boutique or department store on beautiful crystal dishes with gold-washed metal, marble or milk-glass bases, or sets containing soap dishes, toothbrush holder, and drinking glass. There are antique shops with lovely old soap dishes.

But you will get more satisfaction from creating a beautiful box from a scrap, one that has special significance for the recipient, a box that will be treasured long after the soap has disappeared. If you are the kind of person who must create to be happy, you are, no doubt, a hoarder of odds and ends you hope to use some day in some creative way. You have a scrap bag. There is a way to add to your collection. In any community quantities of materials are going to waste in factories, department stores, supermarkets, and other places of business. Generally, it is yours for the asking or for a fraction of its cost. Look in the Yellow Pages of your telephone book and consider what the various firms might have to offer. Then go to see them; don't telephone.

The scraps that furnished materials to cover and decorate the boxes shown in this book were accumulated over a period of time from many sources. The discard barrel of a tannery produced pieces of leather; snakeskin came from a bankrupt shoe factory; a plastics factory contributed scrap plastic; a bag of scrap felt was a buy from a craft shop; several discontinued Christmas-card order books came from a stationery store along with plastic-covered greeting-card boxes; and books of discontinued wallpaper patterns were donated by a paint store.

In addition to the leather, felt, snakeskin, wallpaper, and plastic material from the sources mentioned, boxes were painted, covered with metallic paper, or sprayed gold or silver. They were decorated with plastic fruit, wallpaper, felt flowers, gold-paper medallions, metal foil, lace-paper doilies, papier-mâché flowers and butterflies, a rose made of cornstarch and salt modeling material, and a snowman made of a wallpaper paste and sawdust mixture. You will find recipes for making and directions for using these mixtures at the end of this chapter.

Other decorative possibilities are tatted or crocheted flowers, or medallions, yarn flowers made on an afghan daisy maker, and yarn designs glued to boxes.

The painted boxes were done with Testor's paints from the dime store. They come in ¼-ounce bottles costing $.15 and are available in enamel or flat finish.

Slightly different procedures are necessary when covering boxes, depending upon the shape and material used as a covering. Felt, which I used on several boxes [31], is an easy material with which to work. It can be used on any surface—metal, plastic, wood, or cardboard. Use Sobo glue or Goo on plastic and metal surfaces. Elmer's glue is cheaper and does the job on wood or cardboard. Because felt is more bulky than paper it is usually not satisfactory to turn over edges.

This makes too snug a fit between cover and bottom. A more satisfactory method results when the top and its sides are made in two pieces.

Consider a round box with a cover that extends over the side of the box. Make a pencil line around the base of the cover. Then remove the cover and place it face down on a piece of felt. Draw around the circle. Do this twice; cutting out a top and bottom. Measure the width of the top and cut a band to that measurement and long enough to encircle the box top. Glue on the top and bottom circles making sure they reach the edge. Glue on the top edge. The joining must be snug. Felt lends itself to this method since it can be stretched into place where necessary. The joining should be scarcely noticeable.

Measure the side of the box from the pencil line to

[31]

the bottom. Cut felt to this measurement and long enough to gird the circumference. Glue this to the box, being careful to adhere to the pencil line and also reach the bottom for a snug fit. Ends butted together are less noticeable than those that are overlapped. If the felt is very thick, apply glue to both felt and box. If too much glue is used, it may seep through and show on the outside.

When using paper to cover boxes it is generally easier and more satisfactory to make the cover in one piece. To do this, lay the face of the top down on the paper and draw around it [see Diagram C]. Measure the depth of the side, add ¼ inch to ½ inch to allow for turning under. Add this to the top measurement. Extend the box-top lines to the outer edge. Cut away the corners $\frac{1}{16}$ inch from the pencil line. Then snip into the box corner as shown on the dotted lines [Diagram C]. This allows for a slight overlap at the corners insuring complete coverage. Apply glue to the box top and position it on the paper within the lines. Glue one side at a time, bringing the paper smoothly up against the side and over the edge. Snip the corners where they turn so the paper can be overlapped on the inside when gluing.

Metallic wrapping foil was used on several boxes; it creases easily into place. When box tops completely cover the sides of the bottom section no special attention need be given to the bottom section.

Boxes may be lined with felt or paper using the same procedure as that for making a one-piece cover. They may be painted or sprayed gold.

Tin boxes with narrow rims at the bottom have a more finished appearance when the rims are given a

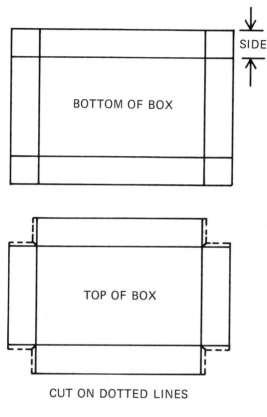

BOTTOM OF BOX

SIDE

TOP OF BOX

CUT ON DOTTED LINES

Diagram C

coat or two of paint before the box is covered to the rims. It is generally easier to paint a hinged box than to cover it. The small well-made appliance box with a spring hinge, chrome trim, and attractive lining is worth looking for because it requires little attention. The box top was given two coats of moss-green enamel; the bottom retained its original white finish.

The cardboard cigar box [32] was given a very different treatment. It was painted flat black giving it a rich, velvety look. Three black-and-white medallions were cut from bathroom wallpaper. They were glued to opaque white plastic cut ¼ inch wider than the medallions. Plastic dots were made with a paper punch. A narrow band of white plastic sets off the rim of the cover.

White paper of good quality, preferably with a shiny finish to contrast with the matte finish of the paint,

[32]

[33]

could be used in place of the plastic. The box holds soap also decorated with the medallions.

Wallpaper may be used to cover boxes if the pattern is not out of scale with the size of the box. Early American calico-like prints or calico cloth work best. There are many attractive adhesive-backed papers from which to choose. Woodgrained and tortoise shell prints make appropriate coverings for boxes that are for men.

Boxes such as the round one with the rose finial can be made from detergent bottles [33]. This bottle was cut off one inch from the top and two inches from the bottom. The screw top was cut off and replaced by a rose made of a salt and cornstarch modeling material. An ornate stopper from a perfume or cosmetic bottle could have been used in place of the rose.

Wrap bars of soap individually before placing in open containers such as saucers and small baskets. This prevents the loss of scent. Bars may also be wrapped in clear plastic encircled with bands of flowers cut from striped gift-wrapping paper, rickrack, yarn, or floral dress tape. Tie several bars in a square of nylon net with contrasting ribbon and a spray of real or artificial flowers for added glamour.

Hand-decorated Paper

Add to that much-sought-after personal touch by hand decorating paper in which you wrap soap or cover boxes. This is a fascinating craft with many possibilities. We will explore a few simple but effective methods and hope they stimulate you to try others. There are many books to consult on the subject.

A quick and effective all-over design can be made by painting the top edge (the thick edge) of a small cookie or hors d'oeuvre cutter with tempera paint. Press the cutter, paint side down, onto the paper. This may be done at random or as a planned pattern [34-1]. Add veins to leaves, flower stems, or other embellishments with a fine paint brush. More than one cutter may be used to make a design.

There are other ways to use a cookie cutter. Flatten a piece of Permoplast. Press the cutter into the surface to a depth of ¼ inch to ½ inch. Remove the cutter and with a penknife or razor blade cut the Permoplast

away from the form, leaving it raised from the surface.
Brush tempera paint over the design and print on paper.
Too much paint will leave a ragged edge; too little a
spotty indistinct print [34-6, 7]. If the cutter is one that
is large enough to be handled comfortably, with the fingers press the cutter through the Permoplast that has
been rolled the depth of the cutter.

Permoplast can also be used in a reverse process by
pressing the cutter into the flat surface, removing it,
then digging out the Permoplast on the inside of the
motif to a depth of ¼ inch to ½ inch. With this
method the outer edge is important. It is the portion
that will be printed. It may be cut into any shape or
pressed into a free form [34-2]. Permoplast takes

[34]

stamp-pad ink very well. It gives a more transparent effect allowing the texture of the paper to show through. Pads are available in several colors. A pad can be made by placing a piece of heavy felt in a saucer and saturating it with ink.

Small calico-like prints can be made with pencil erasers or small corks into which simple designs have been cut with a razor or penknife [34-5]. Soap can be used in place of Permoplast for simple printing. Use soap before it has cured to a brittle stage. Half of a potato or a slice of carrot can also be used for printing. This brings us to printing with a lemon slice [34-3]. This design was made by using the cut side of a lemon half, brushing yellow tempera paint over the surface, concentrating the paint on the rind, center, and ribs and printing. Overlapping yellow lemon slices and green lime slices on blue paper makes a pleasing design.

If you have made soap in the form of leaves or have leaf designs printed or imprinted in the soap, correlate soap and paper by printing leaves. Ink the underside of the leaf for a clear imprint of the vein structure. Leaves inked with a brayer and printer's ink print more evenly than those done with a brush and tempera paint [34-4]. Printing may be done on tissue paper if it is to be used as a wrapping for bars of soap. Stronger paper is needed to cover boxes. An absorbent paper works best.

The paper decorations described so far have been methods of printing. For a different look make paper batik. It is a fascinating craft done with melted paraffin and dye. Plan a simple design on a piece of paper strong enough to remain intact after a thorough wetting. It may be white or a pastel color. Melt paraffin in a small pan set in a pan of water over a burner. Paraffin catches fire easily and should never be melted directly over a burner. With a small brush, wax out the parts of the design that are to remain paper color. Allow a margin inside of areas when applying paraffin. It spreads considerably.

The color of the dye used should be darker than the paper if you are using a pastel color, or it should be one that will combine with the paper color to produce another color, such as yellow over blue to make green. Mix the dye according to directions. Half a package is sufficient. The dye container should be large enough so the paper can lie flat on the water. Cool the dye bath. Hot water would melt the wax and ruin the design. Place the design face down on the water without overlapping. It is difficult to separate layers of wet paper without tearing. Remove the paper when the dye has come through to the back side. Dry it on folded newspaper.

If the paper is strong enough to take another dipping, wax out parts of the dyed portion and dip in a second color. For a two-color batik see [35-1]. This design was made on white paper with yellow dye for a first dipping, then orange dye.

A simplified batik using only one dyeing can be done by using melted crayon for the color. This makes more colors possible. Use the same method as above, waxing out any parts of the design that are to remain paper color. Then proceed by brushing on melted crayon mixed with a little paraffin for easy handling. The paper shown in [35-4] was done by this method. Green and yellow crayon were used on a white background. The design was dipped in red dye.

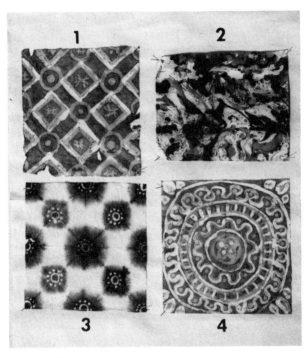

[35]

A combination of batik and tie-dye can be done with folded paper, dye, and paraffin. There are many ways of folding paper. For a simple one, fold a square of paper into a triangle. Continue folding to get smaller triangles. Unfold the paper and mark intersections of creases with a pencil. This gives positions on which to apply design. Design [35-3] was made by painting paraffin dots in a circle around the points of intersection. The paper was refolded and the points dipped in dye. The dipping was shallow to allow for spreading of the dye. Brown dye was used for this design.

Remove wax from designs by pressing the paper between sheets of newspaper with a warm iron.

Marbleized paper is a method of decorating with a decided surprise element that tempts one to go on and on to see what the next piece of paper will produce [35-2]. You need a large pan containing several inches of water, a stick, and oil paints. Tube oil paints thinned to a pouring consistency or enamel paints can be used. Enamel will produce a surface with a high gloss. The small bottles of Testor's enamel need no thinning. They are very convenient since the paint can be poured from the bottles. Wax crayons shaved into turpentine and allowed to dissolve can be used in place of oil paints.

Plan a color scheme that includes dark and light colors with black for accent. Spoon or pour colors upon the water; they will float forming a film. Swirl or make zigzag lines in the water with a stick or pencil to agitate the color into patterns. Do not overmix; this will produce muddy colors. Lay a piece of paper flat upon the water. When the design can be seen through the paper lift it straight up by two edges to prevent blurring. Flip it right side up before placing it upon several thicknesses of newspaper to dry. As you add more color to the water it will build up to produce a more compact pattern. The colors may become muddy, necessitating a change of water.

Ready-mixed gold or silver paints, or powders mixed with turpentine may be floated upon the water. For a more pronounced pattern use the spatter method after the marbleized paper is dry. Dip a stiff brush, such as a toothbrush, into the metallic paint. Shake off the excess paint, turn the brush bristle side down. Scrape a knife blade across the bristles. Experiment before spattering on the marbleized paper. Too much paint on the brush will result in unsightly large blobs. Metallic paint adds a richness to the design that makes marbleized paper an excellent covering for boxes. Use black, browns, and yellows for a tortoise shell effect.

RECIPES FOR ART MIXTURES

Wallpaper and Sawdust Mixture

2 cups fine sifted sawdust
¾ cup dry wallpaper paste

Enough water to make a pliable mixture that will hold its shape.

The snowman box decoration [33] was made with this mixture. A large ball for the body was topped by a small ball for the head and pressed into place. Arms were built out slightly. The end of a match was used for a nose. When dry the snowman was given two coats of white tempera paint. Eyes, mouth, and buttons were painted on. The hat was made from the cup of an egg carton. The scarf is a piece of printed cloth fringed on the ends.

Papier-Mâché

The flower and butterfly decorations were made by applying wallpaper paste between six layers of newspaper [36]. (Colored newsprint could be used.) For a

[36]

two-part flower cut two circles, one slightly larger than the other, from the newspaper while it is still wet but after it has set enough to prevent the pages from slipping. Make flower patterns. Trace them onto the circles and cut out the flowers. Bend the petals upward and place them in a container that will support the petals until they dry. For two-part flowers be sure the bottoms are flat for gluing together. Give the dry flower parts several coats of enamel for a high gloss. It is easier to paint the parts before gluing together.

For a whimsical touch add a chenille bee from the florist shop or a bug pin from the dime store.

Salt Modeling Material

½ cup table salt
¼ cup cornstarch
¼ cup water

Mix ingredients thoroughly. Cook over low heat stirring continuously and vigorously until the material stiffens into a lump. When it is cold enough to model it can be used. To make a rose start with center, form separate petals, overlapping them as they are pinched around the base.

9. Soap Sculpture

Soap as a medium for carving provides a simple and inexpensive way to satisfy the creative urge. Marble, wood, stone, and granite, the conventional carving materials, are not always available, are expensive, require special tools and equipment, and are difficult to handle. They are the media of the skilled artist. Soap makes it possible for anyone to have a creative experience.

No doubt, children and adults, for as long as soap has been made in solid form, have snitched precious bars from the larder to try their hands at carving. Some of these small sculptures have survived the years. A dog and two puppies are treasured by a woman who played with them as a child fifty years ago. There are small busts of Theodore Roosevelt made by the Eureka Soap Company at the turn of the century to attest to the durability of soap for sculptured use.

In 1924 Procter and Gamble sponsored a national soap-sculpturing contest. There were 150 entries. In successive years the number of pieces grew to several thousands. The contest continued for about eighteen years.

Traveling exhibits of small sculptures in white soap were made available to schools, institutions, and libraries. These exhibits included a set of carvings showing the various stages in the creation of a soap sculpture. In addition to the entries of children, these exhibits included the work of housewives and people of every class and occupation. Some remarkably fine sculptures were produced. New talent was uncovered.

Soap carving continues to be done in the schools, but it is generally confined to the size of a standard bar of soap or at best to several bars joined together.

Soap carving should be given more serious consideration as an art medium by the professional artist. Blocks and slabs of any shape and size are available through the simple act of making the soap. The advantage of being able to color it and to carve it before the soap becomes brittle with age is tremendous.

The standard nine-pound recipe on page 21 will make several medium-size carvings.

Milk cartons are available and especially useful containers if a class is involved in a carving project. The quart size is ideal for standing figures. The head [38] was made by a professional sculptor from terra-cotta-colored soap poured into a gallon-size carton. A half-filled shoe box will produce a good-size slab of soap for relief carving, discussed later. Containers can be made that are roughly the shape of the figure to be carved, thus saving on soap. (See Chapter 6.) However, the shavings can be used again by reclaiming them as discussed in Chapter 1.

In order to give you an idea of what can be done with soap as a carving material I invited Richard Groh, a sculptor friend, to carve a block of soap.

I had poured terra-cotta-colored soap into a gallon-size milk carton and allowed it to age for several weeks.

Declining the paring knife I offered him, he used a large wood-carving knife he had brought along. With the knife, a teaspoon to gouge out rounded portions, and a rag on which to wipe soap from the knife blade he was ready to work.

The first thing he did was to mark features on one edge of the soap block with tempera paint [37]. I had wondered whether someone used to working with stone, which offers great resistance, would find soap too soft to be a challenge or, even worse, impossible as a

[37]

[38]

carving medium. As Richard worked I realized I had no
cause to worry. Other than an occasional grunt of satisfaction and a remark about the ease of carving soap,
he worked silently while I took pictures of the various
stages of the carving.

Two hours later the strong, simple head of a woman
was finished. We placed it on a block of dark-stained
wood. At present it is a handsome addition to my book
shelves.

As you have noted the tools and equipment used by
Richard Groh are few and simple. You need a knife

for the preliminary rough carving, the size depending upon the carving. Generally, a paring knife will do. Use a penknife with a small pointed blade for fine work. Add to this one or two orangewood sticks and an old metal tray or box lid to catch the shavings.

When choosing a subject to carve there are no end of possibilities. Designs can range from the naturalistic to the abstract. Simple compact forms are best. Spindly projections are easily broken. Avoid birds or animals with long thin necks and legs and long beaks. Don't be too literal in your translation. Let imagination play a part in your planning. A laugh-provoking imaginative creature might be a good subject for a first carving. Whatever the subject decided upon, make several sketches on paper the size of the piece of soap.

[38] was planned with the features lined up on one edge of the soap block, giving it the greatest depth possible.

Hold the final pattern against the soap and outline the figure with a pointed orangewood stick. Press so that the outline comes through clearly. Go over the lines with a felt tipped pen or a brush dipped in tempera paint. The front and top views can also be scratched on the soap depending upon the subject.

The carving you are about to do is called subtractive carving. Part of the original material is removed by cutting it away. Since material removed cannot easily be replaced it is necessary to work cautiously, turning the sculpture often to view it from all angles as you work. Think of it as three dimensional, something you can hold in your hands—a round, not flat shape. Think in terms of thickness and roundness.

When carving small pieces hold the soap as though

you were paring an apple. Rough out the outline by cutting away the corners. Cut away the soap to within ¼ inch of the outline on all sides. Watch the high points and the low points. The high points are those nearest to the surface, the low points are those farther in. Projections such as ears, tail, and nose should not be finished until the end.

Proceed slowly to shape the model until you have worked carefully down to the actual form and carved away the ¼-inch surplus. The model must be completed as a whole. Do not attempt to finish a single part, such as the head of an animal. This will lead to poor proportion. Keep the knife blade clean. A blade gummed up with soft soap will hamper progress. Lines may be scored into the soap with the tip of a knife, for example, a line around a bird's wing. The depth of the scoring depends upon how far the wing is to stand out from the body. The soap is cut away from the scored line leaving a clearly defined edge that may be softened by rounding off in the final stage of carving. When the piece is finished add details such as eyes, feathers, and hair with the point of an orangewood stick.

Interesting textures can be created by making indentations with a blunt, round object. The teeth of a comb or the tines of a fork can be used to produce straight or wavy lines.

If there are surfaces that are to be smooth, allow the soap to dry for several days or longer. Then rub the areas carefully with a soft cloth, finger, or the palm of the hand. Soap can be polished to a high gloss.

If a piece breaks off it can be mended by digging a small hole into the carving and also into the broken piece. Insert the small end of a piece of toothpick into the carving leaving a short bit projecting. Soften soap shavings in a little hot water and apply a little to the openings in each piece. Press the broken parts together. Wipe off any surplus that oozes to the outside. Allow to dry.

For a finished look most sculptured pieces need a base. This may be planned as a part of the whole or be attached later. It can be of soap, wood, or plastic. To join a sculpture to a soap base follow instructions for joining broken pieces. Instead of small holes, dig trenches in both base and carving. Stick pieces of toothpick or matchstick into base and carving. Fill the trenches with soft soap. Press together and dry. A wood or plastic base can be attached to soap with a solution of sodium silicate (water glass) available in drugstores or with Sobo glue or Goo.

If you prefer a soap sculpture that can be framed and hung on the wall as a picture, make a relief carving. It is much like a raised drawing. Begin by choosing a simple subject with possibilities for adding textural details. A fish is an excellent subject because of its basically simple shape and the opportunity to add texture with fins and scales. Birds, especially the owl, are another possibility, as are turtles, flowers, and leaves. Study early-Egyptian stone reliefs for beautifully done hair, feathers, backgrounds, and other decorative details.

To make a relief draw freehand upon a slab of soap or make a pattern on thin paper that can be traced onto the soap with an orangewood stick. Cut a trench around the figure. Then cut away the background so the figure stands out a little above it. This is called a low or bas-relief. Coins, cameos, and medals are examples of this form of carving. If the background is cut away still more, the sculpture is called a high relief.

You will have to decide whether or not to paint your soap carving. Age gives soap the appearance of old ivory. Some carvings are enhanced by this; others need touches of color to bring out the design. Some subjects might best be carved from soap colored when the soap is made. A Buddha, for instance, could be carved of green soap to suggest jade. (See Chapter 4 for coloring information.)

There are many worthwhile art projects involving soap carving. Make a family project of providing soap figures for a Christmas crèche or spend an evening carving Christmas ornaments. Summer-camp leaders will find soap carving a fine rainy-day craft. Scout leaders might employ it in the study of nature. For patients in hospitals, library groups, and shut-ins, soap carving can afford hours of pleasant pastime.

I hope you have great fun and satisfaction whatever you choose to do, whether it be carving or making toilet soap, and if you make and sell all-purpose soap you can be as successful in the endeavor as the Disterhafts who introduced me to the ancient art of soapmaking.

Bibliography

ANGELOGLOU, MARGIE. *A History of Make-Up*. New York: The Macmillan Company, 1970.

BROOKS, CHARLOTTE P. *Soap Making at Home*. Extension Service, University of Vermont, Brieflet No. 617, January 1942.

COLGATE-PALMOLIVE CO., *A Short History of Soap*. New York: June 1968.

GABA, LESTER. *On Soap Sculpture*. New York: Henry Holt and Co., 1935.

HICKS, DAVID. *On Bathrooms*. England: Britwell Books Limited, 1970.

HOGGARD, HOWARD, M.D. *Devils, Drugs and Doctors*. New York: Pocket Books, 1929.

Penwalt Corporation, Household Products Dept. Philadelphia, Pennsylvania.

POUCHER, W. A. *Perfumes, Cosmetics and Soaps*, Vols. I and II. New York: D. Von Nostrand Company, Inc., 1959.

VAN DOREN, CARL. *Benjamin Franklin*. New York: The Viking Press, Inc., 1938.

VERRILL, HYATT. *Perfume and Spices*. Boston: L. C. Page and Co., 1940.

WRIGHT, LAURENCE. *Clean and Decent*. New York: The Viking Press, Inc., 1960.

Some Sources of Supplies

Candle coloring, molds, decoupage material, carving tools, and metal-tooling foil:

>Gager's Handcraft
>3516 Beltline Blvd.
>St. Louis Park, Minnesota 55416

>American Handcrafts
>Located in 41 States

>Nasco House Crafts
>Fort Atkinson, Wisconsin 53538
>or
>Nasco-West
>P.O. Box 3837
>Modesto, California 95352

>Economy Handicrafts
>47–11 Francis Lewis Blvd.
>Flushing, New York 11363

>Sax Arts and Crafts
>1103 N. 3rd St.
>Milwaukee, Wisconsin 53203

>Sears, Roebuck and Co.
>Replaceable blade utility knife

Lee Wards
Elgin, Illinois 60120

Dick Blick—8-cup art melter
P.O. Box 1267
Galesburg, Illinois 61401

Maid of Scandanavia Co.
3245 Raleigh Ave.
Minneapolis, Minnesota 55416

Gifts and Gadgets
3313 Knox St.
Dallas, Texas 75205

Country Kitchen
270 West Merrick Rd.
Valley Stream, New York 11582